WOMEN IN THE MIDDLE EAST AND NORTH AFRICA

WOMEN IN THE MIDDLE EAST AND NORTH AFRICA
CHANGE AND CONTINUITY

Elhum Haghighat-Sordellini

First published in 2010 by
PALGRAVE MACMILLAN®
in the United States—a division of St. Martin's Press LLC,
175 Fifth Avenue, New York, NY 10010.

Where this book is distributed in the UK, Europe and the rest of the world,
this is by Palgrave Macmillan, a division of Macmillan Publishers Limited,
registered in England, company number 785998, of Houndmills,
Basingstoke, Hampshire RG21 6XS.

Palgrave Macmillan is the global academic imprint of the above companies
and has companies and representatives throughout the world.

Palgrave® and Macmillan® are registered trademarks in the United States,
the United Kingdom, Europe and other countries.

ISBN: 978–0–230–10350–4

Library of Congress Cataloging-in-Publication Data

Haghighat-Sordellini, Elhum.
    Women in the Middle East and North Africa : change and continuity /
Elhum Haghighat-Sordellini.
        p. cm.
    Includes bibliographical references.
    ISBN 978–0–230–10350–4 (alk. paper)
        1. Women—Middle East—Social conditions. 2. Women—Africa,
North—Social conditions. I. Title.

HQ1726.5.H34 2009
305.40956—dc22   2009051141

A catalogue record of the book is available from the British Library.

Design by Newgen Imaging Systems (P) Ltd., Chennai, India.

First edition: August 2010

10 9 8 7 6 5 4 3 2 1

Printed in the United States of America.

To the memory of my grandmother Batool Morakkabi, a strong, selfless woman and an independent thinker who believed in nurturing through love and kindness and continues to inspire me today both personally and intellectually.

And to Paul, Justin Arash, and Brandon Ashkan, for their sense of justice, humility, and integrity.

CONTENTS

TABLES

ACKNOWLEDGMENTS

This work, which debunks several myths regarding women's social status in the Middle East and North Africa (MENA) region, is of particular heartfelt importance to me. It integrates my life experiences accumulated from the years I spent growing up in the Middle East, with sociological research performed during the subsequent years of higher education and career building here in the United States of America. This created a unique contrast between what I know from my own observations, starting with my life in Iran during the country's modernization and pre-revolutionary era, and progressing through the political changes sweeping through the MENA region since then. Observing what was being taught to the public through the media and academia, I noticed that the topic of women's status in MENA is often mistakenly portrayed in a generalized fashion that would lead one to believe that the whole MENA region is culturally homogeneous and led by religious belief in Divine Will. Instead, my studies of this region reveal more complex and diverse dynamics based on political, historical, and cultural differences.

The theoretical and ideological background reflected in this book comes from numerous materials that I started developing through many research projects during my years as a sociologist. Five years ago, I decided to incorporate and develop my ideas along with the results of my research into a book that would contribute to a more accurate understanding of the complexity of women's status in MENA. I am attempting to fill a critical gap with a less biased and more objective representation of women's status in the MENA region.

I extend my sincere thanks and gratitude to the many colleagues, friends, and family members who contributed in different ways to inspire, support, and motivate me. Professors Martin

Oppenheimer of Rutgers University, Kurt Finsterbusch, Reeve Vanneman, and A. Lynn Bolles of the University of Maryland, were my original mentors who inspired me to develop a strong sense of intellectual leadership and insight that I am thankful for. The work and publications of Professor Maria Patricia Fernandez-Kelly, Princeton University, have always been an inspiration and helped me to reflect in a critical way on women's work and their social status in the developing world.

Since joining Lehman College, City University of New York, as a professor of sociology, many of my colleagues have been generous in their friendship and support of my work to bring this book to completion particularly Professors Kofi Benefo, Barbara Jacobson, and Madeline Moran, with whom I am lucky to work with, who have continuously supported and encouraged me. I thank Dr. Anthony Garro for his support of my work. His guidance and direction, while Provost at Lehman College, was critical during the early stages of this book.

I am most grateful to my long-time and dear friends and colleagues at the Graduate Center of the City University of New York, Middle East and Middle Eastern American Center: Dr. Anny Bakalian and Professor Mehdi Bozorgmehr for their unconditional support and twenty years of sincere friendship. I am indebted to them for their help and encouragement in publishing this work.

On the eve of publication, I would like to acknowledge Dr. Farideh Koohi-Kamali of Palgrave Macmillan Press for her professionalism and who expressed enthusiasm in publishing the book. Cindy Nelson, with her experience in editing manuscript, was instrumental in helping me to prepare this book for publication. The artwork used on the cover is a copy of an original painting by the Iranian American artist Simin Massoudi Meykadeh. Her generosity in granting me permission to use her work is appreciated.

And I want, finally, to thank my husband Paul and my sons Justin Arash and Brandon Ashkan for their continuous support while I was tirelessly working on this book over the past several years.

Elhum Haghighat-Sordellini
New York, U.S.A.

PART I

INTRODUCTION AND BACKGROUND

CHAPTER 1

INTRODUCTION

To most of the Western world, the Middle East represents mysterious and exotic cultures, the heart of the world's petroleum production, the birthplace of Judaism, Christianity, and Islam, and the center of today's political and religious turmoil and anti-American sentiments. Although the Middle East is thought to be home to the majority of the world's Muslims, actually, most Muslims live outside of the Middle East and North African (MENA) region. Over a billion Muslims live in about forty-five Muslim-majority and some twenty Muslim-minority countries. The Muslim world spreads from Senegal to the Philippines with the largest number on the South Asian subcontinent; Indonesia is the most populous Muslim country in the world. The mass media of the West portrays the region encompassing the Middle East and North Africa as the heart of the Muslim world, the land of Muslims par excellence, and yet the MENA region contains fewer than twenty Muslim countries and only 20 percent of the world's Muslim population. As table 1.1 indicates, most of countries that have populations of 90 percent or more Muslim are located in Asia and Africa. Albania is the only Muslim majority country in Europe and there is no Muslim majority country in the Americas. In 2005, the largest population of Muslims in the world resided in Indonesia with 88 percent of its 240 million people being Muslim. Indonesia, Pakistan (97 percent Muslim), Bangladesh (85 percent), and Nigeria (50 percent) are among the world's

Table 1.1 Muslim population by country or territories (all values in %), grouped by region. Muslim population subdivided by category, based on available data

Muslim population	Africa	Asia	Europe/North America/ Latin America
90 or more	Algeria, 99 (Sunni 97, Shiite 2) Comoros, 98 Djibouti, 94 Egypt, 94 (Sunni 90, Shiite 2) Libya, 98 (Sunni 96) Mauritania, 100 (Sunni 100) Mayotte, 99 Morocco, 99 (Sunni 99.7) Senegal, 94 Somalia, 100 Tunisia, 98 (Sunni 99.7) Western Sahara, 100	Afghanistan, 99 (Sunni 84, Shiite 15) Azerbaijan, 93 (Sunni 29, Shiite 67) Bahrain, 100 (Sunni 30, Shiite 70) Cocos Islands, 57 Gaza Strip, 99 Iran, 98 (Sunni 10, Shiite 88) Iraq, 97 (Sunni 32–37, Shiite 60–65) Jordan, 95 (Sunni 80, Shiite 15) Kuwait, 96 (Sunni 60, Shiite 30) Maldives, 100 Oman, 99 (Sunni 14, Shiite 4) Pakistan, 97 (Sunni 77, Shiite 20) Qatar, 95 (Sunni 76, Shiite 5) Saudi Arabia, 100 (Sunni 89–90, Shiite 10–11) Syria, 90 (Sunni 74, non-Sunni Muslim 16) Tajikistan, 85 Turkey, 99 (Sunni 83–93, Alevi 7–17) United Arab Emirates, 96 (Sunni 81, Shiite 15) Yemen, 99 (Sunni 70, Shiite 30)	
70–89	Gambia, 87 Mali, 80 Niger, 87 Sudan, 72 (Sunni 70)	Bangladesh, 85 Indonesia, 88 Kyrgyzstan, 76 Lebanon, 70 (Sunni 23, Shiite 38, Druze 7) Turkmenistan, 89 Uzbekistan, 88	Albania, 70

Continued

Table 1.1 Continued

Muslim population	Africa	Asia	Europe/North America/ Latin America
50–69	Chad, 50 Guinea, 69 Nigeria, 50 Sierra Leone, 50	Brunei, 67 Malaysia, 52	
30–49	Burkina Faso, 44 Ethiopia, 35 Guinea-Bissau, 38 Nigeria, 45 Tanzania, 30		
10–29	Cameroon, 22 Ghana, 15 Ivory Coast, 25 Liberia, 21 Malawi, 16 Mauritius, 17 Mongolia, 9.5 Mozambique, 13 Suriname, 14 Togo, 16 Zaire, 10	India, 11 Israel, 12.5 Singapore, 18.3	Bulgaria, 11 Cyprus, 18.5 Yugoslavia, 16
0.5–9	Equatorial Guinea, 0.7 Fiji, 8 Gabon, 1 Kenya, 6 Madagascar, 2 Reunion, 2.4 Rwanda, 8.6 South Africa, 1.2 Uganda, 6.6 Zambia, 1 Zimbabwe, 0.9	China, 1.5 Hong Kong, 0.5 Kampuchea, 2.4 Philippines, 6 Sri Lanka, 8 Taiwan, 0.5 Thailand, 4 Nepal, 5	Canada, 0.6 France, 1 Greece, 2.5 Guyana, 9 Romania, 1.2 Trinidad & Tobago, 6.5 United Kingdom, 1.4 United States, 0.6 Panama, 4.5

Sources: CIA World Factbook (2003); Roudi-Fahimi, *Islam and Family Planning* (2004), table 1, p. 2; Weeks, "The Demography of Islamic Nations" (1988), http://I-cias.com/e.o/sunni.htm, and also from http://go.hrw.com/atlas/norm_htm/srilanka.htm, retrieved on August 11, 2005; http://go.hrw.com/atlas/norm_htm/africa.htm.

ten most populous countries, and will remain so until the year 2050 based on estimates (World Population Data Sheet, 2009). The majority of the world's Muslims (about one in five or close to 20 percent) reside on the African and Asian continents and nearly 20 percent of the world's population is Muslim.

The region identified as the Middle East does not have clear-cut borders. It roughly encompasses the region where Europe, Africa, and Asia meet. The term "Middle East" was used by Western historians and geographers to describe the area from Mesopotamia to Burma. The terminology is perceived as Eurocentric although today it is often used by both Europeans and non-Europeans. The term *Mashreq* (literally means "the East" in Arabic and Persian) is used exclusively in Arabic language contexts and often viewed as the correct one by the Arab-speaking population.[1]

North African countries, due to their strong ties to the Middle East, in addition to recent twentieth-century political events, are frequently grouped with the Middle East and the combined area is often referred to as the MENA region. The World Bank, the United Nations, and other international agencies often use MENA or SWANA (South West Asia and North Africa) when referring to these clusters of countries.

Turkey and Cyprus are often excluded from the classification of South West Asia or even the Middle East. They are considered culturally and politically European because their ties to Europe are stronger than their ties to the Middle East. Azerbaijan, Georgia, Turkmenistan, Armenia, Uzbekistan, and Tajikistan are currently viewed as European countries, and part of the regional bloc in the Caucasus region, because of their strong historical ties to the Russian Empire and the former Soviet Union. However, sometimes they are categorized as Middle Eastern.

The two primary denominations of Islam are Sunni and Shiites (the distinctions between the two are explained later in this chapter). The majority of Muslims are Sunni. Shiites constitute about 10–15 percent of Muslims around the world (Armanios, 2004). Most Muslims in Iran (88 percent), Iraq (60–65 percent), Bahrain (70 percent), and Azerbaijan (67 percent) are Shiite (see table 1.1). Sizable populations of Shiites also live in Afghanistan (15 percent), Jordan (15 percent), Kuwait (30 percent), Lebanon (38 percent), Pakistan (20 percent), Saudi Arabia (10–11 percent), United Arab Emirates (15 percent), and Yemen (30 percent). Although most Muslims in the world belong to either the Sunni or Shiite branches of Islam, a small percentage of Muslims in Algeria, Libya, Oman, and Tanzania identify themselves as Zahirite and Kharijite (Omran, 1992).

The origin of the Shiite-Sunni schism stems from disagreements over the rightful successor to the Prophet Mohammad who died in the seventh century (632 CE). Mohammed and his followers believed that he completed the succession of prophets in human history following Noah, Abraham, Moses, and Jesus. He refined the message of God, which updated and expanded the Old and New Testaments. After Mohammed's death, his followers split into different groups and communities over disagreements about who should be the next person to take over the political leadership of Islam.

Some believed that the position should be given to Ali, Mohammad's cousin and son-in-law (husband of Mohammad's daughter Fatima). This would preserve the leadership through Mohammad's bloodline. They argued that aside from being his faithful and trusted son-in-law, Ali's blood ties with Mohammad and his prominent role as Mohammad's most dedicated and loyal follower qualified him for the leadership position.

Other followers of Mohammad argued that Ali did not have seniority in the hierarchical Arabian tribal system and therefore Abu Bakr, the caliph or the tribal leader, was the most qualified to be the next leader. Abu Bakr was also a trusted friend, companion, and follower of Mohammad. These disagreements led to wars between Ali's and the caliph's followers. The wars ended with no agreements or solutions. The two opposing groups created their own branches. The followers of Ali and his successors were named Shiites (in Arabic meaning supporters of Ali). The others, supporters of Abu Bakr and his successors, were called Sunnis, meaning followers of Mohammed's customs, way of life, or *Sunna*.

Despite the arguments over leadership, the core of Islamic jurisprudence for both Sunnis and Shiites originates from (i) the Quran—the holy book, (ii) the Sunna—prophet Mohammad's life and customs, and (iii) the Hadith—the prophet and his successor's verbal interpretations. The Shiite Hadith and Sunni Hadith are not exactly the same and can differ in context (see appendix A for further explanation of sunnism and shiism and map 1.1 for geographic distribution of both).

Map by Tracy Allen Smith.

DEBATES ON GENDER ISSUES IN THE MIDDLE EAST

The Western media and a substantial body of academic literature portray Islam as the "secluder" and "excluder" of women from the public domain—inhibiting women's integration into the modern workforce, the political sphere, and other aspects of modern life. This Orientalist view[2] paints Middle Eastern women as submissive and powerless, living in a gender-segregated world. The negative image of Muslim women is also partially due to what I call the "bundling effect"—Muslim women are bundled into an undifferentiated group of powerless individuals with no voice, no identity, and no autonomy. Part of the problem is that many Westerners see all Muslims as fundamentalists. Most fundamentalist religious groups are subject to homogeneous stereotyping, and the women in those groups are also lumped together. Some Westerners do not extend their thinking to realize that just as there are many different types of practicing Jews and Christians, there are many types of practicing Muslims—and attitudes toward women and their roles in society vary among all religions. Jewish and Christian women are less frequently stereotyped as one homogenous group; their images in the media are less biased than their Muslim counterparts. Oppressive practices such as polygamy, mandatory veiling, early marriage, multiple pregnancies, and large families are often noted as features of the Islamic culture and religion while in reality these practices are not exclusively Islamic and in fact they are also practiced by Christians, Jews, and Hindus. Physical segregation by gender is often practiced by orthodox Christian, Hindu, Jewish, and Muslim communities. Veiling and all forms of physical covering for modesty is mistaken for an Islamic tradition but in reality veiling manifests itself in all major religions, even prior to Islam (Ahmed, 1992). Female genital mutilation has been practiced mostly in the non-Muslim region of the African continent but is mistakenly mentioned as a Muslim "tradition" (Lockhat, 2004). On the African continent, it seems it is not so much about being Muslim or non-Muslim as it is a cultural practice that spans many faiths and probably happens culturally among nonbelievers as well. And last, the tradition of polygamy is publicized as an Islamic practice, when in fact it is also practiced by some evangelical Christian and certain Mormon denominations.

Unfortunately, the statistics and current media coverage of Muslim women do not help improve the overall image of their status in society. Muslim majority countries are outliers in gender relations, employment patterns, and other demographic factors. With certain exceptions, they generally have lower than average levels of female employment and higher than average levels of fertility and mortality relative to non-Muslim nations at the same level of economic development (Weeks, 1988; World Bank GenderStats, 2006). For example, in 1998, the percentage of females in the labor force in the MENA countries was 27 compared with 42 for other developing nations[3] (World Bank GenderStats, 2006). Among many of these countries, other demographic factors, such as fertility rates, mortality rates, and women's educational attainment, reflect the same disparity.

However, in a growing body of recent academic literature, conventional assumptions about the reasons for Muslim women's disadvantaged social position are being challenged. This body of scholarship rejects the notion that Islam is inherently a misogynist religion, more so than Christianity or Judaism. The scholars argue that the patriarchal social dynamics of Muslim culture support and encourage an interpretation of Islamic doctrine that benefits men's rights (enforced by male elites) and promotes unequal practices for women. Furthermore, it has been in the best interest of the male elites to promote this interpretation.

Scholars such as Kandiyoti (1988) and Caldwell (1982) refer to the power of culture rather than religion in shaping behavior in the so-called belt of classic patriarchy. The Mediterranean and Middle Eastern region that defines the "belt" is characterized by patrilineal extended families. Women are almost always dominated by men, marry young, and are expected to bear many children, especially sons. Restrictive codes of behavior associated with family honor and *sharm*[4] are directly connected to female virtue.

In the work of scholars such as Barlas (2002), Mernissi (1991), and Mir-Hosseini (1999), there is an emphasis on the textual reinterpretation of the Quran. They argue that Islam is wrongly accused of being a misogynist religion. Their premise is that the

Quran, like any religious text, can be and has been interpreted and reinterpreted for the benefit of those in power. Many of the scholars in this intellectual school of thought reject the Western attack on Islam. Leila Ahmed (1992) in her book *Women and Gender in Islam, Historical Roots of a Modern Debate* examines women's positions in different Arab contexts from ancient to modern times. She states that the changing perspectives throughout the centuries were products of the dominant male elite in different Arab countries; the male elite dominated the discourse and patriarchal norms and values were connected to the textual interpretation of Quran. Ahmed, in her analysis of whether Islam improved women's status concludes that the answer is both a "yes" and a "no." If women's status in the "Jahilia" (pre-Islamic) period was in a continual decline, then she attributes the advent of Islam with protecting women's status by virtue of having stopped the downward spiral. It is notable that at the beginning of his prophecy, Mohammad disapproved of the immorality of those who lived in Mecca as well as the rich who dominated the lives of the poor. It can be inferred that the pre-Islamic tribal patriarchy dominating the lives of women must have been equally disturbing. Ahmed then points out how after the Quran was written down, an initial period of interpretation ("ijtihad") transpired resulting in the final law. Further interpretation was supposedly outlawed. Ahmed's thesis is that Islam only helped women by stopping the decline of their status, and that through modern times, the interpretation of Islam has continued and resulted in changes, both good and bad, for women's status. Following the death of Mohammad, Ahmed finds examples of Islam being interpreted at the expense of women's status in order to rationalize the misogynist lifestyles of the caliph and the ruling class. The Arabian tribes, through successful wars of conquest, began to acquire wealth and ownership of property thus leading them to tailor their interpretations for their own convenience. Ahmed adds that the influx of slaves may have created the acceptable concept of human beings as property to be dominated, which helped the patriarchal system to flourish at the expense of the improvement in women's status.

Fatima Mernissi, the Moroccan feminist, stresses a similar interpretation. Her book *The Veil and the Male Elite: A Feminist*

Interpretation of Women's Rights in Islam (1991) explores the influence of the male elite's view on the textual interpretation of Quran. She refers to the type of Islam practiced in Saudi Arabia as "petro-Islam." In the context of this book I will examine how oil wealth has harnessed the power of Islam, and how Islam has harnessed the wealth gained from oil. Saudi Arabia is the example of choice. The analysis of the effects that oil wealth had and continues to have on Islam is a complex subject where political, military, religious, and cultural lines intersect. Saudi Arabia, the ancestral center of Islam, experienced an internal struggle with its Islamic identity. The Wahhabi reform movement of the eighteenth century fought to restore all laws and lifestyles to those established in the beginning of Islam era (800–950). They considered all changes to Islam after 950 null and void. Expelled from Medina, Saudi Arabia, the founder of the Wahhabi sect, Muhammad ibn Abd al-Wahab, converted the Saud tribe to Wahhabism. A holy war (jihad) ensued resulting in the conquest of neighboring tribes by 1763. By 1811 the Wahhabis ruled all of Arabia. Their power was lost due to the intervention of more powerful Egyptian forces and then by 1833 it was restored throughout the Persian peninsula (Algar, 2002).

The discovery of the massive oil reserves, with its vital importance to the West for both economic and military growth, represents the major source of revenue for Saudi Arabia's government. The ruling family and the oil industry control the nation's wealth, and the ruling family's fundamentalist Islamic beliefs control the population (particularly women) breeding an interdependence of petro-wealth and Islam. Petro-wealth has allowed Saudi Arabia, since its birth as a recognized nation in 1932, to expand its influence through the direct export of Wahhabism (Beinin and Stork, 1996; Encyclopedia of Islam and the Muslim World, 2004). Saudi Arabia, through direct foreign assistance, is able to exert political influence on other parts of the Islamic world. The Saudi government, in its effort to spread the influence of Islam, finances the construction of Wahhabi schools and mosques in countries both in and outside the Islamic world. For example, the largest mosque in Europe is located in Rome, home to Roman Catholicism and fully financed by Saudi Arabian government.

Wahhabism has grown from an obscure sect to become mainstream Islamic teaching on all continents. Wahhabist's influence became possible with the petro-wealth accumulated in the twentieth century. Their continued existence relies and will continue to rely on the ability of the Saudi ruling family to control the population, which it has done, so far, through money and Islam (Algar, 1996; Beinin and Stork, 1996; Encyclopedia of Islam and the Muslim World, 2004). The Saudi Arabian elite legitimize discrimination toward women and misogynous practices in the name of Islam.

Stowasser (1998) and Hatem (1998) focus on postcolonial Egypt and stress that the involvement of female religious figures in textual interpretations of Islam made a positive difference and benefitted women's rights. Monira Charrad (2001) examines women's status in postcolonial Algeria, Morocco, and Tunisia. She points to differences in each country showing that they are due not so much to Islam but to the processes of state building that each country experienced, which in turn produced different family laws affecting women's status.

The Overlap of Civil and Family Status Laws

In the majority of Muslim countries civil law and personal or family status law are intertwined. The legal/family system's approach to promoting gender equality is directly related to the influence of the Sharia in the Islamic world.

The civil law often reflects a Western European legal system. For example, the civil legal system in a country such as Morocco is influenced by the French, Spanish, and Portuguese legal systems due to its history of French, Spanish, and Portuguese colonialism, whereas, family and personal status law is built upon Sharia and tribal and ethnic customs of the particular region. The civil law protects and provides for equal status for women, but it is often superseded and overpowered by Sharia in nonsecular Muslim countries.

Sharia is the divine law of Islam that leads Muslims to a "proper and acceptable lifestyle." Sharia has been revised and updated over the centuries and has become a fixed part of the political, social, and cultural reality of the Muslim world. Social legislation almost always derives from Sharia and almost every aspect of ideal conduct is spelled out in Sharia. The laws govern inheritance, marriage, divorce, child custody, family financial maintenance, taxation, fasting, and prayers. Depending on the degree of secularization of a Muslim country, Sharia can have more or less of an influence on the civil law. Countries such as Turkey and Tunisia are an exception in the Muslim world because of their secular nature and unitary governments.

Any changes to Sharia must be done by a *Fatwa* (Islamic ruling) operationalized by higher religious authorities.[5] The Sharia manifests itself differently across the Muslim world, which often hinders women's quest for equal status based on Western standards. Successful reforms in contemporary Muslim countries have been spurred on by women's movements and family-friendly Islamist movements. Iran and Morocco are among the more recent examples, however, the 1979 Iranian revolution led by Ayatollah Khomeini overturned more the liberal aspects of family law that had been in place during the Shah's regime. Feminist Islamist groups were able to gain some equal rights years after the 1979 revolution, mainly in the area of marriage contracts and women's rights in child custody and divorce. In 2004 Morocco's conservative family law was overturned and it was replaced with more liberal family law, which gave women more rights.

Tension in the Muslim world is exacerbated by repressive family law still practiced in some of the countries combined with a civil legal system devoid of protection for women's rights. Here are some scenarios that illustrate women's lack of legal support that the rigid Islamic elite insist on enforcing:

1. Marriage is considered an agreement between two extended families (not two individuals). An Islamic marriage contract may or may not require the consent of the bride but does require the consent of the father or male guardian of the bride.
2. Women have to gain the permission of their male guardians to seek employment, establish a business, or travel alone. Never-married women have to present the permission of their male guardians to be permitted to marry.

3. Divorce can be effectuated by repudiation and does not require a judicial decree. After the divorce, the husband has no financial obligations to provide for the wife. Divorce makes no provisions for alimony.

4. Men have the right to divorce unilaterally (i.e., without his wife's consent) without cause and outside of a court.

5. Polygamy is allowed for Muslim men. He may take up to four wives as long as he is able to treat and provide financially for all of the wives and their children equally.

6. *Sigheh* or temporary marriage is allowed for Shia men and there is no limit on the number of temporary wives that men can have at one time.

7. Women are not granted custody of their minor children even after the death of the father. The guardianship is granted to the paternal male members of the children such as the children's grandfather or uncle.

8. Children's citizenship and religious status is only recognized through the father.

9. Honor killings are often justified and men are acquitted or most likely receive reduced sentences.

10. Women's inheritance rights are lesser than that of men and are often half of their brothers' simply because they are females.

In the process of nation-building and state formation, Islamic countries have to confront the unequal status of women. Some of the Muslim countries have succeeded in improving gender equality and improving women's rights in the areas of education, health, and family law (e.g., divorce, child custody, polygamy, inheritance) by reducing the influence of Sharia and, by extension, mitigating some of the tension between the modernizing and the traditional Islamic elites. But in other Muslim countries disparities continue to plague women. Some examples of the differences follow:

1. In 1975, under Mohammad Reza Shah's regime, Iran's sanction of polygamy was revised limiting men to a second wife, conditional on the court's permission *and* the permission of the first wife. The Family Protection Act that essentially

retained the provisions of the early enactment of 1967 was revised in 1975 to raise the age of marriage from fifteen to eighteen for females and from eighteen to twenty for

males (Joseph & Najmabadi, 2005; Mir-Hosseini, 1993). Women also gained more rights to petition for divorce. For example, a woman could initiate divorce if her husband married another woman without her consent (Joseph and Najmabadi, 2005). With the 1979 Islamist revolution, there was a major rollback of reformed family laws. With the pressure from the conservative religious elites, the Islamists revoked the Family Protection Act and rolled back the clock on the legal improvements that Iranian woman had gained in 1975. Among the more outrageous changes was reducing the marriageable age of girls to nine years (Joseph and Najmabadi, 2005). The Islamists also made veiling mandatory—another rollback and a demonstration of the government's repressive attitude toward women and women's rights (Mir-Hosseini, 1993, 2000; Moghadam, 1994).

2. Tunisia is considered one of the most progressive countries promoting gender equality in marital relations. The Family and Personal Status Code applies to all citizens regardless of their religious affiliation. According to the Tunisian personal status code, a man cannot divorce his wife without grounds (repudiation is not accepted). The divorce has to be obtained through the courts and either spouse is entitled to compensation, especially when the divorce will impose a harmful financial and emotional outcome on one of the spouses. The care and well-being of any children in a marriage is the joint responsibility of both parents. In the case of a divorce, the court will determine custody, taking the children's best interest into account (UNDP, Arab Human Development Report, 2005).

3. In Morocco, adult women are considered independent individuals free to make decisions. In legal matters, a woman can designate adult male members to negotiate on her behalf and can even represent herself. Therefore, a woman can negotiate a marriage contract on her own without the consent or involvement of a male family member. In a divorce case, both

husband and wife have equal legal rights. Divorce provisions for the husband often involve bringing two reputable witnesses to testify on his behalf. Reconciliation is an important part of the divorce procedure, especially if there are children involved. If the reconciliation attempt fails, a sum of money will be allocated to pay for the children and the wife's maintenance. Women can initiate divorce if it is written into the marriage contract. But they can also initiate a divorce based on emotional, financial, and moral injuries (e.g., abandonment, violence).

4. In Algeria, family law still heavily favors men. There have been some positive changes in recent years such as constraints on polygamy. The husband has to obtain the permission of the first wife and prove that he is able to continue providing equitably for his wives and children. Also, among the latest achievements is the equal right of Muslim women to marry non-Muslim men. A marriage between a Muslim man and a non-Muslim woman was considered legitimate and legal while the marriage of a Muslim woman to a non-Muslim was not. With the passage of this law regarding mixed marriages, women are recognized to exercise the same rights as men.

5. In Kuwait a women's legal status is limited and unequal to men. Polygamy is acceptable for up to four wives and even permissible for more than four if the husband divorces one of the wives. One important provision in the recent Kuwaiti family law has been to prohibit a man from bringing a second (as well as third) wife to live in the home of the first (or other) wife. He has to be able to provide separate households for each wife and their children (UNDP, Arab Human Development Report, 2005).

A study of marriage contracts in different parts of the Middle East indicate that an increasing number of women are stipulating provisions in the contract to protect themselves during the marriage and in the event that the marriage is dissolved. The stipulations range from prohibiting the husband from practicing polygamy, awarding custody of the child to the wife in the case of divorce, ensuring that alimony and child support will be provided, and so forth (Mir-Hosseini, 2000). Women often use their dowries (*Mahr*) to improve their position without any legal stipulations. For example, *Mahr* can be used as a negotiation tool. In the case of divorce, a woman is entitled to have her *Mahr* returned. A woman might forgive her *Mahr* with the condition that she will be entitled to half of her husband's estate (Hoodfar, 1996). Some women forgive their *Mahr* to gain custody of their children at the time of divorce or "buy out" the husband (Mir-Hosseini, 2000). Changing the family law regarding equal inheritance for women has been one of the most difficult challenges. Families that are inclined to treat their daughters equally often find loopholes in Islamic law. "For example, a father may make a pro forma sale of a portion of his assets to his daughter, or he may divide up his wealth among his children while he is still alive" (UNDP, Arab Human Development Report, 2005: 135).

ATTITUDES TOWARD THE SEPARATION OF RELIGION AND GOVERNMENT

With respect to the separation of religion and government we need to be aware of a fundamental difference between the histories of the West (North America and Europe) and the MENA region.

The very first attempt to colonize North America was motivated by the people's desire for freedom from a state religion. The pilgrims fled Europe to escape religious persecution and oppression by the Church of England, the Anglican Church, which was the state church. By intertwining the Church of England with the government, both the church and the state controlled the people. As colonies developed into the United States of America with a central Federal government, this original mission of freedom from religious obligations (forcing the people into or away from a religion) was incorporated into the very first amendment of the Constitution. Over the next two centuries, the effective separation of church and state was cemented with further clarifications.

The idea that any religious teaching should never be forced on the people through direct control of the government by the church is one of the foundational blocks of American history and culture and as a result is ingrained in the American educational system. Indiscriminately assuming that the separation of church and state is the standard to which all other societies should be held contributes to the concept of Orientalism (refer to endnote 2 for further explanation of Orientalism). In other words, if people are not alert to this, it could be easy to assume that separation of religion and government is a universal concept naturally occurring in the development of all societies.

Europe started out with a political system in which the government was indistinguishable from religion. The results were state mandated religions and laws based on the leader's interpretation of religious texts. However the seeds of an eventual separation of church and state were already visible in the *Magna Carta* issued in the 1200s. The realization of a true separation of church and state continued to gain momentum and became part of the Western culture with Martin Luther's doctrine of the two kingdoms and John Locke's principle of social contract. The most accurate description of the concept can be summed up by quoting James Madison (the principal drafter of the U.S. Bill of Rights), who claimed that a total separation of church and state would guarantee the purity of both.

Many of the MENA countries that are examined in this book bypassed the Western experience of separating religion from governing powers. While in the West the effects of religious culture on politics is clearly visible in the historical developments, in the MENA region we find that even in present times political policies are often directly dictated or strongly influenced by religious leaders. Under Islamic governments, religion and state are not separate entities and political life exists within the context of Islamic law. Islam provides the broader context in which the state operates, but laws are also devised by the state that are not explicitly taken from religious writings; rather they are derived from an interpretation of the religious writings.

As a result, nations formed along the two different paths: secularism in the West versus religious control of law in the MENA region. As societies in the MENA region progressed toward modernization, the outcome has been very different from what was anticipated given the Western model (there is an extended discussion of modernization theory in chapter two).

Countries in the MENA region underwent modernization with all power over the people originating from leaders who ruled through divine right granted by the interpretation of Islamic texts. This helps to explain how pre-Islamic patriarchy did not change dramatically even when countries went through periods of great wealth, modernization, urbanization, and industrialization as seen starting in the oil development period that began in the twentieth century. With few changes in the patriarchal structure of these societies, modernization did not have the anticipated positive impact on women's social status and their participation in the workforce, despite the statistics on reduced fertility and increased education.

WHY ISLAM ALONE IS INSUFFICIENT TO EXPLAIN WOMEN'S STATUS IN THE MENA REGION

Women's roles in Muslim societies, women's status, and women's rights, or lack thereof, are entangled in a complicated patchwork of social customs, Sharia, civil laws influenced by Western European legal precedents, and the influence of the relatively recent influx of oil wealth common to many Middle Eastern countries. The goal of this book is to debunk some common assumptions about women's educational progress, fertility, work opportunities, and social status in the Muslim Middle East and North Africa.

Debunking, as the famous sociologist Peter Berger (1963) explains, entails demystifying behaviors by examining the layers of complex social structures that lead to those behaviors. It requires exploring the interrelationship of multiple factors that influence women's integration into public life—factors such as fertility, education, employment, and labor migration. It necessitates examining the impact of sudden oil wealth on developing countries. It involves looking at the complex ways in which patriarchal systems are intertwined and often embedded in Islam and enforced by predominantly male dominated governments. I argue that while Islam is a powerful cultural, religious, and political force it certainly is not the sole factor contributing to the subjugation of women's rights in the MENA region.

This book takes us through a historical and sociocultural journey and examines the economic, cultural, and demographic transformations of the region from an historical perspective and notes the social forces that have transformed the region over the past several decades. The focus of the book will be on why it is important to study demographic factors such as women's entry into the modern workforce.[6]

Middle Eastern women's social transformation toward more personal independence and a fuller integration into both economic and political life is a reflection of not only the economic and political changes in modern societies but also changes in their cultural practices, gender relations, and society's demographic characteristics. It is not a simple process, by any means. Women's integration into the workforce, lower fertility rates, and higher educational attainment is a consequence of women's decreasing poverty, higher standards of living, and increasing numbers of women who feel empowered to pursue their own agenda. Amartya Sen (1999) makes a convincing case in his studies of South Asian and other less-developed countries: "Societies need to see women less as passive recipients of help, and more as dynamic promoters of social transformation . . . suggesting that the education, employment and ownership rights of women have a powerful influence on their ability to control their environment and contribute to economic development" (qtd in Lopez-Claros and Zahidi, 2005: 3).

In conducting this study, I reference eighteen countries with a majority Muslim population and that are traditionally included in the region designated as the Middle East and North Africa. The countries include—North Africa: Algeria, Egypt, Libya, Morocco, Tunisia; Persian Gulf States: Bahrain, Kuwait, Oman, Qatar, Saudi Arabia, United Arab Emirates, and Yemen; the rest of the Middle East: Lebanon, Iran, Iraq, Turkey, Syria, and Jordan.

This study uses a macro-level, multidisciplinary approach and does not emphasize any specific country. It examines the region's similarities and differences in terms of demographic characteristics. The book's focus is on the countries that are bound by the Islamic religion mostly speaking Arabic, with the exception of Iran and Turkey where Persian and Turkish are the official languages. Since I am trained as a sociologist, I naturally gravitate toward studies in my own discipline, although I have tried to make this study a multidisciplinary work by including the work of anthropologists, demographers, economists, feminists, historians, policy experts, political scientists, and psychologists.

APPENDIX A: DIFFERENT BRANCHES OF ISLAM

Shiism and Sunnism can be further subdivided into different branches. Each branch has its own school of thought and Islamic jurisprudence. The different branches of Shiism include:

1. *The Twelvers* or *Ethna Ashari Shiism*: The Twelvers accept the descendents of Ali (twelve including Ali) as the infallible Imams that are from the bloodline of Prophet Mohammad. The last Imam, Mehdi, also referred as the "hidden Imam," is viewed as the one who "disappeared" in late ninth century and is expected to return someday to lead the community of Muslims. The Twelvers are considered the largest community of Shiites. They reside mainly in Iran, Iraq, Syria, South Lebanon, Bahrain, Pakistan, Afghanistan, and India.

2. *The Seveners* or *Ismaili Shiism*: The Seveners agree that Ali was the Imam succeeding Mohammad but disagree on successors of Ali. They consider the son of the sixth Imam, (Jafar al Sadeg) whose name was Ismail, as the last Imam (the Twelevers however believe that Mirza al Qazim, the other son of Jafar al Sadeg was the last Imam). Since the Seveners' seventh Imam was named Ismail, their group is called the Ismailis. Today, the Seveners are clustered in Afghanistan, Iran, India, and Pakistan as well as in East and southern Africa, mainly in the Zanzibar region of Tanzania (Omran, 1992).

The *Druze* are a derivative of Ismaili Shiites. They are small in number and their religious practices are often viewed as considerably different from mainstream Shiite Islam. Most Druze practices are kept among their community and they are considered a closed community scattered in different parts of the Middle East (Armanios, 2004).

3. *The Zaaydis*: The Zaaydis recognize the first five Imams but reject the existence of the "hidden Imam" Mehdi. They mainly reside in the northern region of Yemen and a smaller community of Zaaydis lives by the Caspian Sea region in Iran.

4. *The Alawites*: The Alawites are a small group mostly settled in Syria and Lebanon. They are known as an eclectic group celebrating Christian and Islamic holidays and viewed as a private and secretive group in their interpretation and practices of Shiism. Alawites study the Quran and follow the five pillars of Islam, but also incorporate elements from other religions that have passed through the region historically.

5. *The Alavis*: The Alavis (like the Druze) are a derivative of Shiite Islam. They are spread throughout Turkey and are socially and politically well integrated into Turkish society (Armanios, 2004).

Within Sunni Islam, there are four schools of legal thought, jurisprudence, or *fagh* guiding the majority of Muslims in different parts of the world:

1. *The Hanafis*: The Hanafis are considered the oldest school of thought (among the four Sunni schools) founded by Abu Hanafi. Abu Hanafi (699–767 CE) was the first Islamic philosopher who systematically compiled and documented Islamic law. The Hanafis were prominent during the Abbasids dynasty that ruled Iraq, Turkey, and Iran for almost five centuries (from the eighth to thirteenth centuries). Today, they are prevalent in Turkey, Central Asia, the Balkans, Iraq, Syria, Lebanon, Jordan, Afghanistan, Pakistan, Bangladesh, and India.

2. *The Malikis*: The Malikis are mainly located in North Africa (mainly Mauritania), the Arabian Peninsula (mainly Kuwait and Bahrain), and the Andalus (Arab Spain) as well as in Western Africa and western Sudan. The Malikis are considered the second largest of the four schools of Sunnism. The beginning of the Maliki school of thought originates back to Imam Malik (715–796 CE).

3. *The Shafeis*: The Shafeis are prominent in many parts of the Muslim world including Egypt, Iraq, Syria, Sudan, Ethiopia, Somalia, and parts of Asia such as Indonesia and Malaysia. The Shafeis are one of the four major schools in Sunni Islam, founded by Imam Shafei (767–820 CE).

4. *The Hanbalis*: The Hanbalis are a prominent and powerful group in Saudi Arabia, Qatar, some parts of Oman, United Arab Emirates, and was started by Imam Ahmad Ibn Hanbali (780–855 CE). It is the fourth major school in Sunni Islam.

CHAPTER 2

THE PATH OF SOCIAL AND ECONOMIC CHANGE ACCORDING TO THE MODERNIZATION THEORY

Much of the Middle East and North Africa gained independence from Western European imperialism and foreign rule shortly after World War II. The influence of European colonialism, however, was supplanted by the growing influence of the United States and the former Soviet Union. After the fall of communism, the United States emerged as the dominant foreign power in the Middle East and through its reach into the oil industry it contributed to the political turmoil that had been smoldering since the 1940s. The region experienced rapid economic development during the 1950s, and the oil boom of the 1970s contributed to further economic, political, and demographic changes. With oil prices soaring in the 1970s, "it was like drawing the winning global lottery ticket; from being the poorest countries in the world, the Gulf States found themselves among the wealthiest" (Hijab, 1988: 36).

The rapid rise in wealth from oil revenues created rich governments that became the main political and economic powers in the region. In addition to the political turmoil, the region experienced a population explosion and rapid economic development. There were significant demographic changes resulting from an influx of foreign labor, rural-urban migration, and rapid urbanization. Much of the Middle East can be characterized as functioning with a predominantly patriarchal structure, and although patriarchal structures are resistant to social changes, the growing modernization and urbanization of the region still managed to lead to important transformations in gender roles.

Modernization theory is a predominant theory that explains the path of social and economic change. The following sections will introduce ideas and concepts related to the theory of modernization and begin to explore the disparity between projections for the MENA region based on the theory and what has actually happened in this region.

MODERNIZATION THEORY

During the 1950s—the post–World War II era—when the Western world was flourishing economically, the modernization perspective provided the dominant theory for explaining the ways in which a society could reach economic prosperity. Modernization was described as a process of transition: a society goes through one stage and enters another. The evolution begins with the society in the preindustrial agriculture stage, it then moves into an industrialized, urbanized stage, and later on to the postindustrial stage. Countries are defined as "modern" based on their degree of industrialization (Inkles and Smith, 1974; Moore, 1979; Parson, 1971). Modernization is also a process that transforms (i) a society's intellectual and technological properties, and (ii) helps the members of the society take greater control of nature and their environment (Black, 1966; Black and Cottrell, 1981; Levy, 1966; Rustow, 1967).

During the transition, modernization theorists argue that new ways of life, which subsequently change a society's values and norms as well as its demographic characteristics, develop; the occupational structure of the society changes and educational opportunities for its citizens increase. Changes such as these can bring more opportunities and comfort to women's lives, especially when they are followed by reduced fertility and household responsibilities. Interestingly, women's participation in the labor force declines during the early transitional stages (from preindustrial agriculture to industrial manufacturing economy) and picks up momentum when the society enters the postindustrial service economy[1] stage. As the formal labor market grows during the early stages and agricultural sector jobs decline, more women leave agricultural work. However, the absence of jobs for women in the early manufacturing economy leads to an overall decline in women's employment. (Anker and Hein, 1986; Boserup, 1970; Oakley, 1974; Ryan, 1975; Tilly and Scott, 1978). Later on, with job growth in the service and white-collar occupations, women's labor force participation increases again (Evans and Timberlake, 1980; Kentor, 1981; Semyonov, 1980). The transition from a preindustrial agriculture economy to an early industrial urbanized economy, and later to postindustrial economy, is explained by modernization theorists as having a U-shaped effect on women's labor force participation. Thus, there is a *curvilinear* rather than a *linear* relationship between economic development and female employment (see Boserup, 1970; Haghighat, 2002, 2009; Oppenheimer, 1970; Pampel and Tanaka, 1986).

When women's employment declines during the transitional stage—from a preindustrial agricultural to an industrial economy—changes are also taking place with respect to their households and family responsibilities. In preindustrial societies women are able to combine housework and child care with market work (i.e., petty trade, carpet and basket weaving, small-scale farming). Industrialization and urbanization divide the home and work spheres (work is done in an urban setting removed from the domestic residence). Because the domestic responsibilities remain primary to women, the physical separation of work and home lives limit their opportunities to participate in the market. Therefore, their rate of participation in the labor force declines (see, e.g., Anker and Hein, 1986).

During the later stage of industrialization—post-industrialization[2]—women have benefited from more education, and declining fertility rates. Couple that with more job opportunities and women's participation in the labor force increases (Jelin, 1977; Nash and Safa, 1976; Semnoyov, 1980; Wilensky, 1968). Evans and Saraiva (1993) refer to this stage as the expanding opportunities hypothesis:

> the expanding opportunities hypothesis claims that women's labor force participation should rise during industrialization because there will be rapid growth in demand for workers in

traditionally female occupations such as garment production and because urban, industrial life expands women's educational opportunities and undermines repressive attitudes toward women. (P. 26)

As women gain more access to the labor market in industrial and later in postindustrial economies, they tend to join the service sector more than any other sector and frequently join traditionally feminized occupations.

MODERNIZATION AND ITS EFFECT ON TRADITIONAL VALUES

Modernization theorists[3] claim that as the modernization process evolves in a society, it creates more favorable conditions for women to enter the labor force. Therefore, women's workforce participation increases with a higher degree of industrialization and urbanization (Durand, 1975). Social and cultural changes such as delaying marriage, declining fertility rates, and an increasing demand for a more educated labor force, all contribute to a larger supply of female workers. With the help of modern technology and smaller family size, women are freed from overburdening domestic responsibilities (i.e., early marriage, subsequent pregnancies, child care responsibilities, and housework) and are therefore more available to be employed.

Modernization also brings potentially beneficial changes in values and lifestyles for both men and women. The traditional values and ways of life, characteristic of premodern societies, are replaced with less traditional, more rational, and more flexible life choices (see Weber, 1958). Ting-Toomey (1999), for example, distinguishes between past-oriented and future-oriented values. She states that a culture based on past-oriented values is static. The focus is on maintaining an active connection with historic and ancestral ties. A culture open to future-oriented values yields a dynamic society that reacts to change by establishing objectives for growth. Another example is illustrated by Sanderson and Alderson (2005). In describing the societies that are still in the premodern phase, they state that past-oriented societies lack a kind of *mentality* that promotes development. Future-oriented mentality on the other hand is connected to rational, future-oriented values and ethical systems. There is less of an emphasis on past traditions and customs and more on future changes (p. 192).

However, others argue that modernization does not necessarily have to change people's belief systems and values to a more "modern" way of thinking. Traditional values can operate side-by-side with a modern lifestyle and intellectual well-being. For example, DiMaggio's work (1994), based on the theoretical premises of Karl Marx (1973), and Daniel Bell's work (1973, 1976) argue that with modernization people's belief systems do not necessarily convert to a modern and more rational way of thinking. A society's cultural heritage *can* stay intact during the process of economic development, modernization, and urbanization, and even after the process has been completed. Others such as Inglehart and Baker (2000) make similar arguments. In their study of the waves of the *World Values Survey*, which canvassed sixty-five countries representing 75 percent of the world population, they identified some countries that underwent both modernization and a radical change in culture while other modernized countries maintained their pre-modernization cultural inheritance. They emphasize that cultural change is not automatic during modernization, but "path dependent." While wealth and technology may contribute to modernization, the history of the country's cultural path determines cultural change. They argue that a society's cultural heritage (e.g., Protestant, Confucian, or Muslim) leaves an imprint and influences subsequent societal change:

> values seem to be path dependent: A history of Protestant or Orthodox or Islamic or Confucian traditions gives rise to cultural zones with distinctive value systems that persist after controlling for the effects of economic development. Economic development tends to push societies in a common direction, but rather than converging, they seem to move on parallel trajectories shaped by their cultural heritages...the fact that a society was historically shaped by Protestantism, or Confucianism or Islam leaves a cultural heritage with enduring effects that influence subsequent development. Even though few people attend church in Protestant Europe today, historically Protestant societies remain distinctive across a wide range of values and

attitudes. The same is true for historically Roman Catholic societies, for historically Islamic or Orthodox societies, and for historically Confucian societies. (P. 49)

CHALLENGING THE CONVENTIONAL MODERNIZATION PERSPECTIVE

There is a significant weakness in the modernization perspective; although widely applied, it has not been able to explain women's status and the demographic changes influencing their lives in some parts of the world, particularly in the Middle East. Ester Boserup's work *Women's Role in Economic Development* (1970) challenged modernization and particularly the perspective that technology liberates women and therefore has positive consequences on women's status. She argued that urbanization (as a consequence of modernization) encourages rural-urban migration and therefore creates a less favorable situation in urban areas for women to be employed. Women are often cut off from the kinship support networks they belonged to in rural settings. Transfer to the urban setting is less favorable to women migrants due to the loss of the rural kinship network. Before leaving the rural farm life, women could count on multigenerational kinship support in case of illness, child care, household duties, and shared financial support of the family. Once they left that environment for the urban life, they were alone or with a husband, with fewer or no extended family in the vicinity for support, and also had to purchase all social services (daycare, health care, and housing). Furthermore, as reported by Luo (2005), while a change in the economy made it favorable for women to migrate and enter the workforce, persistence of the traditional cultural barriers to women subjected them to significant wage discrimination.

Boserup has argued that in preindustrial societies there is a positive correlation between women's status and their roles in food production. In agricultural rural communities women contributed extensively to food production as primary farm workers. As industrialization advanced and societies were introduced to new technologies, women were marginalized from agricultural work. Boserup examines the economic situation of women in cities and notes that they were often excluded from formal sector jobs in modern sectors due to their low levels of education and discriminatory practices. Many activities that were traditionally done by women were taken over by men in the modern sector. With modernization and improved technology in farming, women's status declined since their contribution to the family and the rural economy decreased. Thus with industrialization and technological advancements women in urban area are more marginalized from economic involvement. Urbanization in fact marginalizes women not only from economic involvement but also from the kinship support networks that were available to them in farm communities.

Other perspectives have been offered to explain the lack of women in the workforce in the Muslim Middle Eastern countries. For example, the sociocultural perspective explains women's lower participation in the modern sector—regardless of a woman's qualifications or a demand for labor—as a result of powerful gender relation cultural norms, particularly the strong kinship system, the patrilineal descent tradition, and patriarchal norms that discourage women from entering the labor force and participating in the modern sector of the economy.

Chapter three looks at some of the variants of modernization theory and begins to introduce some of the analysis of prominent Middle Eastern scholars on the unique attributes of the MENA region. Chapters three and four will also begin to look at the effects of the global economy on women's work experiences, as well as the issue of women's status as defined by their level of empowerment. In the end, it is appreciating the combined effect of these influences that helps us understand the particular experience of Middle Eastern women as they struggle to elevate their status and become integrated into the modern economy and the workforce.

CHAPTER 3

PATRIARCHY, MODERNIZATION,
AND THE GLOBAL ECONOMY

WHAT IS PATRIARCHY AND HOW MUCH
INFLUENCE DOES IT CARRY?

Studies of ancient societies suggest that patriarchy was institutionalized with the rise of urban societies (Ahmed, 1992; Lerner,
1986). The phenomenon of "the creation and establishment of
patriarchy" was a process "developing over a period of nearly
2500 years, from about 3100 to 600 B.C. Patriarchy occurred
even in the Ancient Near East, at a different pace and at different
times in several distinct societies" (Lerner 1986: 8).

The first urban centers in today's Middle Eastern region
arose in Mesopotamia around 2500 BC. Hierarchical, class- and
gender-based societies continued to develop in different parts of
the world. In those societies "the patriarchal family, designed
to guarantee the paternity of property-heirs and vesting in men
the control of female sexuality, became institutionalized, codi-
fied, and upheld by the state" (Ahmed, 1992: 12). Eventually,
with the shift from feudalism to capitalism in Western Europe,
patriarchy was replaced by a new system. Gender inequality and
traditionalism were replaced by modernism (Lerner, 1986),
which supported a lesser degree of gender inequality.

Patriarchy is considered a system that enables men to dominate women and maintain the power and control of resources.
Women—especially younger ones—have minimal power and

are dependent on men (Cain et al., 1979; Mason, 1986). Kandiyoti (1992) defines classic patriarchy as a systematic unequal position of women in societies. She describes a patriarchal family as multigenerational and hierarchical, where younger women and children are placed in the lowest level of the hierarchy. The *paterfamilias,* as she calls it, is characterized by young women marrying men older than themselves (frequently significantly older). When the young bride enters the new household, she is placed at the lowest level of the hierarchy with the least amount of power. Upon bearing sons, she gains more status and eventually, by becoming a mother-in-law, she gains more power as an older female in the household. Marrying young girls is important because it legitimately extends the length of time that they can bear children. A young woman is also more readily socialized to their unequal role and inequitable entitlement to the family resources—even compared to their own children (Kandiyoti, 1992; Moghadam, 2004). Women's modesty and the practice of veiling, *Hijab* or *Purdah,* is also emphasized in patriarchal societies. Within a community, a woman's honor is an extension of the family's honor and reputation. What do women gain from their lower status with these inferior arrangements? In exchange for their low status and unequal access to resources, women are entitled to protection and maintenance. Kandiyoti (1992) refers to this exchange as the "patriarchal bargains."

Johnson (1997) describes four dimensions of a patriarchal social structure. He argues that these structures are:

1. Male domination—men predominantly hold the most prestigious and powerful roles and women hold the least powerful roles.
2. Patriarchal control—women are devalued and experience physical, psychological control, violence and fear of violence in their everyday lives because of the ideological need for men's control, supervision, and protection.
3. Male identified—most aspects of society that are highly valued and rewarded are associated with men and identified with male characteristics. Any other attributes less valued and rewarded are associated with women.

4. Male centricity—public attention (e.g., the media, public spaces) is often granted to men and women are placed in the background and on the margins.

Hughes et al. (1999) describe patriarchy as an institution where gender inequality is perpetuated by a set of complex processes referred to as sexism:

> The most pervasive form of institutional sexism is patriarchy, a system of social organizations in which men have a disproportionate share of power. Patriarchy is rooted in cultural and legal systems that historically gave fathers authority in family and clan matters, made wives and children dependent on husbands and fathers, and organized descent and inheritance through the male line. (P. 250)

THE INFLUENCE OF PATRIARCHY ON WOMEN'S EMPLOYMENT

On the demand side, patriarchal values embedded in the culture discourage employers from hiring women and investing in them (e.g., Papanek, 1990). Therefore, societies with strong patrilineal descent and strong extended family and kinship systems (e.g., Middle East, South and East Asia) tend to keep women out of the labor force. If women are included, they will be employed in lower paying jobs where men are given better and more prestigious jobs (see, e.g., Greenhalgh, 1985; Jones, 1984; Pyle, 1990; Salaff, 1981). Youssef (1974), for example, in contrasting the labor force experience of women in the Middle East and Latin American countries, states that "the level of economic development does not explain the extent to which women participate in the non-agricultural labor force" (p. 21).[1] She places greater emphasis on the kinship system and social organization of the family. She links the low proportion of women in modern sectors, to the cultural norms in Islamic societies that stress restricted and limited interaction between women with non-kin male members. Papanek (1973) analyzes the seclusion of women in the Muslim and Hindu societies through their "separate worlds," and the "symbolic shelter" of women who are seen as vulnerable to the outside world and in need of protection by the male members of their family.

Cross-national research by Clark et al. (1991), among others,[2] posit that regional differences in culture and traditions have a stronger influence on women's employment statistics than economic development. They argue that the scanty representation of Middle Eastern women in the labor force is a result of the Islamic ideology of secluding women and the traditional support for a patriarchal system. When they included Latin America in their study, their analysis found that women in Latin American countries and women in Middle Eastern countries were substantially less likely to participate in the labor force than women elsewhere. They argue that the influence of Islam, with its ideology of secluding women and Catholic Latin America because of its cultural and ideological support for a patriarchal system, have inhibited women's entry into the paid labor force.

In general, these studies perceive the less rigid kinship structure of non-Muslim countries as more adaptable to demographic changes, such as the higher demand and greater opportunity for female employment that may accompany economic development. It is argued that since Islamic doctrine encourages the separation of the sexes and a clear division of labor, as well as a patriarchal family system, women are not encouraged or invited to enter the paid labor force. The literature also portrays Muslim women as being submissive to the Islamic patriarchal structure that has been historically embedded in the region (Altorki, 1986; Moghadam, 1988; Walter, 1981). Since women's formal employment (as well as low fertility and higher educational attainment) are considered as some of the main indicators of higher status of women in the society, it is argued that women in Muslim as opposed to non-Muslim societies have lower status (Caldwell, 1982; Clark et al., 1991; Marshal, 1985; Youssef, 1974). An ideology that supports the isolation of women therefore inhibits their admission into the formal labor force regardless of the country's level of economic development. While I would agree that Islamic ideology in the context of social history of the region promotes separation of the sexes and contributes to the sustained low status of women, I will argue that it is the governments' active role in implementing and protecting this ideology that is the real mechanism by which women's status is controlled.

PATRIARCHY MEETS MODERNITY: THE NEOPATRIARCHY PERSPECTIVE

Although in the Western world patriarchy has been replaced by a lesser degree of gender inequality, Sharabi (1988) argues that patriarchy in the MENA Arab countries has also changed; it has become modernized but not in the manner of Western modernization. He refers to this phenomenon as neopatriarchy. Neopatriarchy tries to explain the discrepancy between industrialization and the absence of an increase of women in the workforce. With respect to gender roles, neopatriarchy defines a woman's primary role as homemaker and mother (not far removed from traditional patriarchy). Therefore, changes in the level of industrialization have little effect on women's involvement in the market; industrialization and modernization do not change women's participation in the labor force. Furthermore, neopatriarchy argues that in the process of becoming modernized, some of the oil-producing Arab countries experienced a rapid economic development that did not follow the economic development path of Western nations. This perspective views the process of modernization as a uniquely European phenomenon (Sharabi, 1988). Only Western societies experienced modernization in a "pure" sense because it happened without interference from other nations. Due to their dependent political and economic positions and their cultural differences, modernization in today's developing countries would not follow the path of the Western nations.

Sharabi (1988) expresses the two main concepts of neopatriarchy as being (i) patriarchy (cultural), and (ii) dependency (economic). Its economic structure is dependent capitalism[3] and its social structure is patriarchy. Neopatriarchy is the product of the interaction between modernity and patriarchy (tradition) in the context of dependent capitalism. In neopatriarchal societies, there is a wide gap between inward and outward societal context. Kinship and culture in these societies are deeply rooted in patriarchal values (inward) even with the presence of modern forms of government and economic development strategy (outward). Sharabi states: "A neopatriarchal society is incapable of performing as an integrated social or political system, as an economy, or as a military structure. Possessing all the external trappings of modernity, this society nevertheless lacks the inner force, organization, and consciousness, which characterize truly modern formations" (pp. 6–7).

Sharabi describes being modern as a state of mind (psychological changes) embracing structural changes and processes (political and economic changes) in the society. He does not romanticize modernization nor consider it superior, but considers modernization as a "mode of being." To Sharabi, a modernized society has three characteristics: modernization, modernity, and modernism. Modernization is the process of economic and technological transformations. Modernity is the changes in the structure of the society, that is, political and economic structures that need to change for the society to be considered modern. Modernism is the consciousness or the state of mind appropriate to a modernized society. A neopatriarchal society does not embrace all the changes that are necessary for a modernized society. For example, Saudi Arabia as the largest oil-producing gulf state went through rapid modernization (economic and technological) with only partial gains of modernity and even less modernism.

A neopatriarchal society experiences structural changes under a dependent economic and political system without breaking its patriarchal culture. Thus, "the success of modernization itself is disabling when carried out in the framework of dependency and subordination and resulting in neopatriarchy" (p. 22). These societies, therefore, do not experience the same demographic changes as would be expected of a society approaching "modernization." Slow or no reduction in fertility, mortality, and little or no major sectoral changes in female labor force participation are some of the demographic "imbalances" that might be observed in those societies (see Mabro, 1988; Obermeyer, 1992).

Sharabi explains that in Arab countries, when transitioning to modernity (from patriarchy to modernization), the state

became the central controlling force in society, not just by their monopoly of coercion but also by their vastly increased economic power as owner of the basic industries, source of all major investments, only international borrower, and provider of all essential services...the state became within a few years the largest employer in society. (P. 60)

Sharabi concludes that this strategy became financially possible mainly because of the sudden accumulation of oil revenues and other investment strategies. In neopatriarchal societies, the state then becomes the ultimate power and also the main employer and investor.

In sum, women in the MENA region, from pre-Islamic times through the spread of Islam and continuing through the periods of oil wealth accumulation and global industrialization, continue to find power concentrated in the male domaine (patriarchy). This fact is important in explaining why women's status in MENA has not changed as much as expected regardless of dramatic economic prosperity or failure, advancement in health care and education, the shift toward a global economy, or even in light of global changes in political ideology. Islam simply became another vehicle used to perpetuate male control. And in times of actual or perceived political failure, Islam becomes fundamentalist in nature to legitimize its reaction to destroy any force bringing social change upon the population.

PATRIARCHY AS A POLITICAL AND ECONOMIC EXPEDIENT

Mainstream political views see Islam as a religion that obligates a lower status for women with respect to men for no other reason than Divine Will. As will be mentioned several times in this text, the pressure to maintain the status quo of women in the MENA region stems more from economics and politics, with Islam playing the trump card as needed. Islam provides a government with precedence and a convenient explanation for its control of MENA society and therefore it must be maintained at the core of government regulations in order for the country to survive.

Traditional roles for women are constantly portrayed in the political arena as symbols of traditionalism, Islamization of the state, and in reaction to the interference of Western politics. Moghadam (1993, 2004) applies the neopatriarchal framework to the legal and political status of women in Muslim societies. She writes:

> Neopatriarchal state practices build upon and reinforce particular normative views of women and the family, often but not exclusively through the law. In particular, laws that render women legal minors and dependents of men reflect and perpetuate a modernized form of patriarchy. In some cases, the focus on women is an attempt to deflect attention from economic failures. States may also find it useful to foster patriarchal structures because the extended family performs vital welfare functions. (P. 14)[4]

A similar argument by Obermeyer (1992) focuses on the politics of fertility, mortality, and female labor force participation in Arab Muslim nations and states:

> The ambivalence of any Arab/Muslim leaders toward female emancipation stems from their need to address two conflicting demands in their societies: prosperity, which means modernization; and identity, which is partly rooted in tradition...the traditional bases of identity present themselves as the safest choice, and religion is used selectively to cope with political exigencies and to legitimize the power of individual leaders. (P. 52)

Hijab (1988, 1994) also challenges the mainstream view. She argues that Islam is used selectively to suppress women's rights when it is actually more of an economic decision justified and reinforced by traditional values when that makes the most political and economic sense. She states that conservative attitudes toward women have existed in many parts of the world and in different societies throughout history. She presents studies of countries such as Tunisia and Iraq where the role of the government in social attitudes toward women's employment changed when their labor was in demand. For example, Iraq's need for workers was so pressing that the government imported over a million Egyptians to be employed in the agricultural sector. The Iraqi government also made special efforts to change social attitudes toward women's involvement in the public sector through media and elite channels. Hijab (1988) gives the example of a pharmaceutical plant north of Baghdad where female workers had to be brought in from Baghdad and housed in dormitories because the plant was not able to hire women from the nearby village as local women were not allowed by their male family members to work in the factory. The villagers were resentful of the new plant. Sometimes the buses transporting women from Baghdad were attacked. Gradually, women from the villages started to seek work in the factory themselves, first being chaperoned by their male relatives and finally going to work on their own.

Hijab also cites the example of Tunisia where the government had been eager to integrate women into the modern labor force up until the unemployment of men became a serious problem. She states that the male unemployment problem became so serious that the state could not afford to consider the needs of both men and women. The government "was clearly happy to adopt the traditional view that men were the breadwinners and had to be planned for accordingly, and that women were the economic responsibility of their men folks" (p. 81). In times of high unemployment the government's inability to grow the economy in order to create jobs or provide social benefits replacing women's services becomes the real reason for reverting to "traditional ways." In essence, to avert a sociopolitical crisis due to a failing economy, the government may fall back on the Islamic excuse to exclude women from competing with men for jobs by claiming that traditional gender roles must be preserved. Religion becomes the justification and allows the government to preserve itself by not having to admit its inability to provide jobs and revenue.

There appear to be different justifications regarding the enforcement of religion to inhibit women's entry into the labor force. In some instances, the Muslim elite argue that Islam prohibits women from leaving their family duties and entering the labor force. In other instances when the economy is suffering and unemployment is a problem, the government may use religion, intertwined with patriarchal belief systems, as an excuse to exclude women from the labor force thus protecting men from competing for the same jobs with women. The end result is the same; religion is used to justify a patriarchal system in the face of a failed or failing economy.

To sum up, it seems that once women's labor in the modern sector is in demand, government responds to the need by integrating women into the modern workforce. Islamic ideology as a conservative factor to suppress women's equal access to the modern sectors is manipulated when the society is facing a high rate of male unemployment. Government officials engineer this strategy as a way to deflect attention from economic failures. The state may find patriarchal structures politically and economically useful because the extended family performs vital functions. Gender issues have been addressed in these countries superficially because women's employment has never been seriously in demand. Because of high fertility rates, and political and economic failures, governments are facing high rates of unemployment and a disproportionately young population in search of jobs. In these circumstances, Islamic ideology is manipulated to keep women out of the labor force and men are given priority. Tinker (1990) states:

> When development is rapid, it is inevitable that these changes create tension between sexes and generations and those pressure groups appear that seek to preserve or reintroduce the traditional, hierarchical cultural pattern. This is the case in oil-rich countries in the Arab world, which have attempted to preserve the family system of domesticated and secluded women by mass importation of foreign male labor, and in which mass movements of Muslim revival pursue the same aim. (P. 24)

Up to this point we have touched on the impact of sociocultural, economic, and political forces on women's status. Moving on to global forces, we need to examine the effects the globalization of the world economy has had and will continue to have on women's status. The Muslim nations studied in this book, whether wealthy oil-producing OPEC members or less-developed nations, all have a direct connection to the global world economy. A financial crisis in an affluent capitalist country can have immediate, profound effects on middle or low income countries. Conversely, a popular uprising in a small nation whose oil production can barely maintain the economy can affect the global price of oil and as a result drive up inflation around the world.

THE GLOBAL ECONOMY AND
WOMEN, WORK, AND STATUS

Dependency Theory

Dependency theory, originating from Marxism, proposes that world capitalism has resulted in two groups of countries: the powerful ones who exploit the resources of the less affluent nations and the ones who are being exploited by affluent countries.[5] Based on this thesis, global capitalism helps affluent nations to continue to flourish while low income societies move downward with their societal changes and development. These countries could progress toward economic development but only with the influence of the affluent countries. Cardeso and Enzo (1979) refer to this as *dependent capitalism.*

Frank (1966), in his famous piece "Development of Underdevelopment," proposes that the development of rich societies and their accumulation of wealth are based on the exploitation of other nations and is a way to keep those nations in a less-developed state by exploiting their labor power and raw materials (oil, uranium, diamond mines, etc.). Amin (1974, 1997) refers to "articulated" and "disarticulated" economies. He argues that developed nations have built articulated economies, whereas different institutions and sectors in underdeveloped societies are not as well articulated; that is to say there is only a tenuous relationship between the raw material exported and local manufacturing. In a disarticulated economy, there is no relationship between producers and consumers. That is, producers do not supply an internal market demand and therefore benefit minimally from their own work. A small class of local elite control the production of goods and cooperate with transnational companies/corporations who export the goods, and in the process they accumulate wealth (both the local elite and transnational companies). The local elite are those who profit by creating trade and banking relations favorable to themselves and the foreign clients (multinational companies), but unfavorable to the local population (Roberts and Hite, 2000). Amin claims that the main cause of disparities and inequalities in disarticulated economies is foreign control of those economies.

A major motivator for the globalization of the economy is cost-cutting—the relocation of work from affluent nations to less-developed nations where labor and operating expenses are less. Roberts and Hite (2000) point to a paradoxical effect on women's status when developed nations invest and create jobs in underdeveloped nations. In the beginning they notice that the jobs created yield earning power for women with the immediate effect of improving their quality of life. In addition it provides women with the opportunity for independence, material benefits, and to a certain extent a sense of self-actualization. However women employed in the foreign factories begin to see the disadvantages of working for a transnational corporation as they become marginalized and exploited, often working in oppressive work conditions, with lack of job security and earning low wages.

In general, dependency theorists would argue that the West had exploited and prospered through access to the MENA regions' cheap petroleum production. MENA women would only enter an exploiting workforce if needed and enforced by their country's elite and multinational companies. Since the production and development of the oil industry brought a sudden influx of wealth, countries in the MENA region (some more than others) managed to enforce patriarchal cultural practices channeled through Islam, limiting women's entry into the labor force and keeping their social status at a lower level despite their improvement in education, lower fertility, and lower mortality. In the upcoming chapters we will examine the socioeconomic, political, and demographic mechanisms in place in the MENA region (also see Sharabi's neopatriarchy theory that stems from dependency theory and is developed and applied specifically to oil-producing MENA countries).

World System Theory

World system theorists add to dependency theory and argue that economies create one single unit that does not consist of independent countries and nations as it is often argued (Wallerstein, 1974a, b, 1979, 1980, 1989; Wallerstein and Hopkins, 1996). The unit consists of three categories of countries: core, semi-periphery, and periphery. Core countries are usually the most advanced affluent industrial countries. They are involved in exploiting other countries' resources and goods. Semi-peripheral countries consist of middle income and semi-industrialized societies. Their development is somewhat dependent on the exploitation of peripheral countries and somewhat controlled by core countries.

Peripheral countries are those that are manipulated by core countries. Their industrial and economic development is limited. Proponents of this theory, such as Wallerstein, claim that single societies do not develop in a vacuum but as part of the capitalist world system and

> they exert their effects only in the context of a society's position within the world-system at a particular time in history. As the world-system evolves, there is increasing polarization between core and periphery, and it is difficult for less-developed nations to improve their status, or at least improve it very much. (Sanderson and Alderson, 2005: 201)

Other proponents of this perspective argue that the global division of labor could be beneficial to developing nations by including and offering them opportunities to transform their economies (Evans, 1995). The involvement of multinational corporations in developing nations does not necessarily hurt them. It could stimulate their economic and industrial growth (De Soya and O'Neal, 1999; Dollar, 1992; Firebaugh, 1996, 1999; Hein, 1992).

World system theorists explain economic development in the MENA region as controlled by core countries that limit their industrialization and their integration to the global economy. Oil-producing countries that hold tremendous wealth and can provide an abundance of jobs could be placed in the semi-peripheral category. In oil-producing countries, for example, the stratification and discrimination is multilayered (global as well as local) and is also reflected in the workforce; the higher paying and higher status jobs often go to native male workers (e.g., in Saudi Arabia, UAE, Bahrain) and lower paying, temporary jobs are often reserved for immigrant, temporary workers contracted for a limited number of months or years. Native women are not encouraged to enter the labor force but immigrant women are used as source of cheap labor as domestic workers. Higher paying and higher status jobs such as nursing and teaching could be filled by female professionals, often times from other non-oil-producing Arab countries (e.g., Egypt, Morocco, Tunisia) since these gender segregated societies do have the need for female professionals. In the upcoming chapters (chapters seven and eight), we will examine work characteristics and labor migration to MENA countries and explain these theories further. As we will see later in the book, despite the reduced fertility and higher educational achievement of women in the MENA region, their labor is not utilized and their social status has not significantly improved as might be expected from such advancements.

DIVISION OF LABOR AND WOMEN'S WORK

The previous sections indicate that the modernization theory points to a gradual increase in women's education and employment, and a decline in fertility during the evolution of a society from an agricultural to an industrial base. For example, women's participation in the labor force plummets during the early industrialization phase but grows as the society advances toward more industrialization. A higher demand however, does not necessarily mean better paying and higher status jobs.

In societies that are highly involved in the world economy and the new international division of labor, women are often marginalized in the world economic system, much to their disadvantage, and end up in low paying jobs (see Beneria and Feldman, 1992; Fuentes and Ehrenreich, 1983; Hu-DeHart, 2003; Jain, 1990; Nash and Fernandez-Kelly, 1983; Pyle, 1990; Safa, 2002; Tinker, 1990; Wolf, 1990). Although men are often preferred to women by multinational corporations, these corporations offer menial labor-intensive jobs that are often reserved for young, single women (e.g., Nash and Fernandez-Kelly, 1983; Sassen, 1988). Therefore, economic development might be facilitating women's entry into the labor force but could also marginalize them in the process by exploiting their cheap labor.[6] Women are often left with few opportunities and alternatives and are forced by their poverty to participate in "a system that generates and intensifies inequalities...[and] makes use of existing gender hierarchies to place women in subordinate positions at each different level of interaction between class and gender" (Beneria and Sen, 1982: 290). Thus, it is argued that modernization of a capitalist kind in different parts of the world has not only reduced the economic status of women but also resulted in their marginalization and impoverishment (Sen and Grown, 1987; Ward, 1984).

In sum, as a society progresses toward industrialization, there is no doubt that demographic, cultural, and institutional changes occur. In Muslim societies, the demographic changes have been *inconsistent* relative to what modernization, dependency, and world system perspectives have been able to explain. In the following chapters, we will see how in most of the Muslim world fertility has dropped, educational attainment of women has increased, and mortality rates have declined, but overall, women's social status has not improved as much as has been expected. We will explore the reasons further to shed light on the demographic changes in the region. As table 3.1 reflects on development and demographic indicators of the MENA countries compared with the world and other regions, most MENA countries have made tremendous improvements when it comes to life expectancy at birth and have managed to lower their natural increase and poverty rates. The rates for Gross National Index (GNI) as indicated in table 3.1 vary from one country to another; oil-rich countries report high GNI and oil-poor countries show a low GNI as expected.

Table 3.1 Selected development and demographic indicators of MENA Muslim countries compared with the world and other regions

Country	Population mid-2007 (millions)	Rate of natural increase, 2007	Projected population change (%), 2007–2050	Percent urban, 2006	2006 GNI PPP per capita (US$)	Life expectancy at birth (years), 2006 Male	Life expectancy at birth (years), 2006 Female	Population living below US$ 2/day (%)	Energy use per capita 2002 (kg oil equivalent)
Algeria	34.1	1.7	47	49	6,900	71	74	15	985
Bahrain	0.8	1.8	56	100	18,770	73	75	–	9,837
Egypt	73.4	2.1	61	43	4,680	68	73	44	789
Iran	71.2	1.2	41	85	–	71	76	7	2,044
Iraq	29.0	2.5	114	67	–	55	59	–	1,199
Jordan	5.7	2.4	71	82	6,200	71	72	7	1,036
Kuwait	2.8	1.9	84	98	29,200	77	79	–	9,503
Lebanon	3.9	1.5	27	87	5,460	69	73	–	1,209
Libya	6.2	2.0	57	85	–	71	76	–	3,433
Morocco	31.7	1.5	43	55	5,000	68	72	14	363
Oman	2.7	2.2	42	71	14,570	73	75	–	4,265
Qatar	0.9	1.5	55	100	–	71	76	–	19,915
Saudi Arabia	27.6	2.7	80	81	16,620	73	77	–	5,775
Syria	19.9	2.5	75	50	3,920	71	75	–	1,063
Tunisia	10.2	1.1	29	65	8,490	72	76	7	846
Turkey	74.0	1.2	20	66	9,060	69	74	10	1,083
United Arab Emirates	4.4	1.5	90	74	23,990	77	81	–	9,609
Yemen	22.4	3.2	159	26	920	59	62	45	221
Region*									

Region									
World	6,625	1.2	40	49	9,940	66	70	53	1,669
More developed	1,221	0.1	3	75	29,680	73	80	—	4,878
North America	335	0.6	38	79	43,290	75	81	—	7,946
Europe	733	-0.1	-9	72	22,690	71	79	56	3,614
Less developed	5,404	1.5	49	43	5,480	64	67	59	893
Less developed (excluding China)	4,086	1.8	61	42	4,760	62	65		869
Africa	944	2.4	107	37	2,550	52	54	66	692
Northern Africa	195	1.9	59	50	4,660	67	70	29	773
South America	381	1.5	38	80	8,790	69	76	76	
Western Asia	223	2.0	65	64	8,180	68	72		2,065
South Central Asia	1,662	1.7	56	30	3620	63	64	75	598
United States	3,022	0.6	38	79	44,260	75	80	—	7,943

Source: *World Population Data Sheet.* 2005, 2007. Washington DC: Population Reference Bureau.
MENA: Middle East and North African region.

* Definition of region:
North America: United States and Canada; Europe: Continent of Europe; Africa: Continent of Africa; North Africa: Algeria, Egypt, Libya, Morocco, Sudan, Tunisia, Western Sahara; South America: Argentina, Bolivia, Brazil, Chile, Columbia, Ecuador, French Guiana, Guyana, Paraguay, Peru, Suriname, Uruguay, Venezuela; Western Asia—Armenia, Azerbaijan, Bahrain, Cyprus, Georgia, Iraq, Israel, Jordan, Kuwait, Lebanon, Oman, Palestinian Territory, Qatar, Saudi Arabia, Syria, Turkey, United Arab Emirates, Yemen.

PART II

STATUS AND THE COMPONENT VARIABLES THAT INFLUENCE WOMEN'S ADVANCEMENT IN THE MENA REGION

CHAPTER 4

WOMEN'S STATUS: THE QUESTION OF ACCESS TO RESOURCES AND WOMEN'S EMPOWERMENT

Status equates to a recognized social position that people occupy in societies. It helps people define who they are and their relationship to others. The study of the status of women is an important indicator of the degree of gender equality in a society. It is considered a sociocultural variable that is influenced by social class, religion, race, ethnicity, and age. There are multiple components that add up to a woman achieving status including access to material resources such as land, wealth, jobs, and health care, and nonmaterial resources such as prestige, knowledge, and reproductive control. In a patriarchal family system, men control the resources and therefore maintain power and control of the family (Mason, 1986, 2001). Women in the MENA region have been gaining access to material resources such as education and family planning, however, access to resources is not the only requirement for acquiring power. To acquire power, one needs to have choices. Kabeer (2000), in her thought-provoking article on women's status and empowerment, describes empowerment as the ability to exercise choice in full force:

> One way of thinking about power is in terms of the ability to make choices: to be disempowered, implies to be denied choice...the notion of empowerment is that it is inescapably bound up with the condition of disempowerment and refers to

the processes by which those who have been denied the ability
to make choices acquire such an ability...empowerment entails
a process of change. People who exercise a great deal of choice
in their lives may be very powerful, but they are not empowered, because they were never disempowered in the first place.
(Pp. 436–437)

Empowerment cannot be defined in terms of specific activities
or end results because it involves a process whereby women can
freely analyze, develop, and voice their needs and interests without them being predefined or imposed from above. Therefore,
access to resources is an important aspect of women's access to
power and higher status in societies, but without the ability to
choose what to do with those resources and the ability to exercise autonomous control of the new skills there is no power.

In a study of Lebanese women, Lattouf (2004) examines women's social status in modern Lebanon. Despite their
improved educational attainment, there is a lack of advancement in their social status. Lattouf argues that economic stagnation and regional political problems led the government to
enforce traditional roles and values on women and institute
campaigns to legitimize discrimination against women. This
analysis echoes Hijab's assessment (1988, 1994) of women's
advancement and decline in Tunisia.

A similar study by Shavarini (2006) reveals the same concerns for contemporary Iranian women's social status. Despite
women's impressive improvement in their educational attainment at the secondary and college levels within the past two
decades, they still have a tremendously lower status than men,
and lack opportunities in the job market (the unemployment
rate for women is as high as 20%, whereas for men it is about
12%). Both Shavarini's and Lattouf's observation of why families
support their daughter's higher educational attainment, despite
the questionable rate of economic return, has to do with family
status: A family will support their daughter's higher education
as a way to improve her chances of finding a husband of similar
or higher social status, which, in turn, adds to the family's collective social status. Iranian women's social status, as is the case
in many other societies, is often determined by their relationship to a male relative or husband. Shavarini states that many of

the women she interviewed were aware of societal discrimina-
tions in finding jobs even with their high level of credentials
and qualifications. In an economically deprived country such
as Iran, with a high inflation rate and a high rate of unemployment, men are given priority in access to jobs and therefore
many highly qualified women with college degrees are unable
to find suitable employment. Shavarini (2006) discusses the
paradox of women's higher education in Iranian society:

> What good is their higher education, then, if society cannot
> utilize women's education? What are these women supposed to
> do with that education that has been training them, suppos-
> edly, for a job that will never materialize? The answer to these
> questions is the paradox of women's higher education in Iranian
> society. (P. 207)

The examples of Lebanon and Iran are an indication of how
access to resources is not enough to improve women's social
status, position, and their access to power. According to Kabeer
(2000), access to resources is only one of three criteria that
enable women to advance their social status and power. She
identifies three dimensions of choice that define empowerment:
resources, agency, and achievement. She refers to *resources* (i.e.,
education, health-related services) as a precondition to enhance
the ability to exercise choice and therefore acquire a greater level
of power and social status. *Agency* is the process that defines
individual goals and continues to act upon them. *Achievement*
is the desired outcome where individuals receive the rewards for
their achievements (better employment due to higher education) and therefore are empowered.

The three dimensions of choice leading to power and higher
social status, as Kabeer states, explain why women's higher education (resources) and lower fertility patterns are not enough to
empower them in Iran and Lebanon. If women are educated but
not given much access to political and economic power, the process
of empowerment is not complete and therefore their status stays
low despite higher investment on their human capital. Iranian and
Lebanese societies are two examples of countries where the government has been tapping into and capitalizing on deep-seated
notions of traditional family values to keep women out of the

labor force and political involvements. In reality, their stagnant economies lead to high inflation and unemployment rates; therefore there is shortage of jobs to go around. Men are given priority and the society justifies this process with the rationalization that it is not an economic problem, but rather it is preserving traditional and Islamic family values. The educational opportunities are welcomed by women and their families but women are left with no option for gaining status and power other than vicariously through the men in their lives (husband, father, or brother).

If women's status and power within their families is a function of their attachment to male family members, they can gain power through an exchange of resources (Kandiyoti refers to this as "bargaining with patriarchy"). For example, Kabeer uses an example from her study of Muslim and Hindu women in India. Unlike Hindu women who do not inherit property (inheritance of property is collective and is often passed to sons), Muslim women according to Sharia law are entitled to an inheritance (a woman's share is equivalent to half of her brother's share). Kabeer on the other hand finds that both Hindu and Muslim women are equally property-less even if Muslim women should own some properties through inheritance. She finds that even though Muslim women are given property rights, this does not necessarily mean they are exercised by them. Kabeer's explanation (2000) is as follows:

> Although Muslim women do waive their land rights to their brothers (and may be under considerable pressure to do so), they thereby strengthen their future claim on their brothers, should their marriage break down. While brothers have a duty under Islam to look after their sisters, the waiving of land rights by sisters in favour of brothers finds a material basis to a moral entitlement. The necessity for such an exchange may reflect women's subordinate status within the community but the fact that women's land rights are in principle recognized by their community gives them a resource to bargain with in a situation in which they have few other resources. (P. 444)

DIFFERENT MEASURES OF WOMEN'S STATUS

The status of women in social demographic studies is often measured according to how they rate, relative to men, on the following criteria (this not an exhaustive list):

- access to reproductive health services;
- access to education ;
- female mortality, infant mortality, for example, male versus female life expectancy (ratio of male to female);
- age at first marriage (the higher her age at marriage, higher her autonomy and decision-making ability);
- preference (as well as men's) for sons;
- political participation (i.e., percentage of women in the parliament);
- paid employment (i.e., women's share of the labor force participation).

Among other types of measures commonly used are the systematic measures calculated by the United Nations Development rogramme (UNDP; see table 4.1 for these measures). The two measures of gender status are (i) Gender Empowerment Measure (GEM) and (ii) Gender-related Development Index (GDI). Here is how UNDP describes these two indices:

1. Gender Empowerment Measure (GEM) is a "composite index measuring gender inequality in three basic dimensions of empowerment—economic participation and decision-making, political participation and decision-making and power over economic resources."
2. Gender-related Development Index (GDI) is a composite index measuring average achievement in the three basic dimensions captured in the human development index—a long and healthy life, knowledge and a decent standard of living—adjusted to account for inequalities between men and women (UNDP, Human Development Indicators, 2003).

A low number indicates a high GDI rank. For example, the United States' GDI is 7, which translates to it having a high GDI (women have access to more resources in the United States) compared with a GDI of 148 for Yemen or 126 for Morocco indicating a low access to resources for women.

Table 4.1 Political leadership indicators and GDI in the MENA region compared with other regions

Country	Percentage of women in parliament (1995–2004)		Percentage of women holding ministerial and sub-ministerial ranks (1998)	GDI rank (2003)
Algeria	7	6	5	107
Bahrain	—	0	1	37
Egypt	2	2	5	120
Iran	4	3	1	106
Iraq	11	8	0	—
Jordan	1	6	1	90
Kuwait	0	0	5	46
Lebanon	2	2	0	83
Libya	—	—	5	61
Morocco	1	11	6	126
Oman	—	—	4	79
Qatar	—	—	0	44
Saudi Arabia	—	0	0	73
Syria	10	12	3	110
Tunisia	7	23	8	91
Turkey	2	4	13	96
United Arab Emirates	0	0	0	48
Yemen	1	0	0	148
Region				
World	12	16	11	—
More developed	14	20	14	—
North America	14	17	32	—
Europe	15	20	12	—
Less developed	11	14	9	—
Less developed (excluding China)	9	13	9	—
Africa	9	13	9	—
Northern Africa	4	9	—	—
South America	10	15	12	—
Western Asia	5	6	—	—
South Central Asia	6	9	4	—
United States	11	14	32	7

Notes: Data for Gender Empowerment Measure (GEM) are not available for most of the MENA countries. The top ten countries with the highest Gender-related Development Index (GDI) rank are: Norway, Iceland, Sweden, Australia, U.S.A., Canada, Netherlands, Belgium, Denmark, and Finland.
MENA: Middle East and North African region.

Source: Women of Our World. 2002, 2005. *Population Reference Bureau*, Washington, D.C.; United Nations Development Fund: http://hdr.undp.org/reports/global/2003/indicator/pdf/hdr03_table_22.pdf. Retrieved on August 30, 2007; 2005 World Development Indicators, Women in Development, World Bank.

As useful as these measures appear to be, they have been criticized as not being an accurate measure of gender inequality. These measures are also not available for all countries, particularly many of the MENA countries (see table 4.1). The main critique of these measures comes from Pillarisetti and McGillivray's study (1998) of the indices. Although they acknowledge the importance of these indices to measure gender empowerment and equity from a cross-cultural perspective, they list problems with the measurements as follows:

- These measures of the treatment of inequality aversion are insensitive to differential cultural and social norms across countries (especially between industrialized and traditional developing countries)
- They do not consider some important empirical realities concerning the size of the manufacturing sector in developing countries and the reliability of developing country databases
- They ignore some fundamental variables relevant to empowerment. (P. 202)

WOMEN'S POLITICAL PARTICIPATION, SOCIAL STATUS, AND THE LINK BETWEEN STATUS AND LABOR FORCE PARTICIPATION

There is no uniform evidence throughout the Muslim world to back up the mainstream view of the low status of Muslim women and the injunction with "out of the norm" demographic patterns such as higher fertility, low participation of women in the labor force, and so on. Obermeyer (1992) emphasizes the political dimension of Muslim societies and concludes that "while the subordinate status of women is common to all patriarchal societies, [whether] they are Islamic or Western, in contemporary Islamic societies the link between gender relations and political structures seems more inextricable than it is elsewhere..." (pp. 53–54).

Other similar studies by Jeffery and Jeffery (1997), Iyer (2002), and Bose (2005) in studying South Asian communities find a stronger link between women's autonomy in decision-making with their social class, accessibility to family planning programs, educational attainment, regional and residential differences than with their religious affiliations to Islam, Hinduism, or any other religion.

In sum, if a woman's access to societal resources is the key that gives status, women in the MENA region only have access to a limited number of resources and the question is of why those resources have become available while others have been restricted.

The study of women's status in MENA requires a multidisciplinary approach. The relationship of women to their society in MENA is not a one-dimensional argument where women are facing a single social ideology that opposes change. In order to best use the material presented in this book, there is a need to shed light on the constraints of the current dominant paradigm derived from the limited and narrow focus of popular media. It would be a mistake to examine adherence to the religious doctrines of Islam as being directly responsible for women's status. While I do not deny the fact that Islam plays a role in regulating women's social status, I conclude that it is more important to study how Islam is used as an instrument of control in response to forces originating in the region's cultural history, how the region followed a different path of modernization, and how political and economic realities (domestic and global) took advantage of the region's Islamic roots to control the population in accordance with the needs of the governing elite. While in the West there was a collision between religion and State resulting in their separation and eventual continued progress on parallel paths prior to modernization, in the MENA region, religion is indistinguishable from government prior to, and during, modernization. As a result, in general, when modernization began in MENA, the transformation of women's social status in Muslim societies did not mirror what had happened in the West.

In the following chapters, I will examine women's fertility patterns, education, participation in the labor force, labor migration, and presence of oil wealth, all in relation to the impact on women's status. Through secondary data analysis and case studies of select countries I will explain the dynamics of the changes that occurred in the MENA region and whether or not these changes have advanced women's status.

CHAPTER 5

WOMEN'S STATUS AND
FERTILITY PATTERNS

The direct and indirect effects of fertility patterns on other demographic factors have been studied extensively by demographers. The declining fertility rate in much of the developed world is generally attributed to a complex set of factors related to modernization and economic development.[1] For example, the fertility-female labor force participation nexus generally shows a negative relationship in industrialized societies indicating that as societies modernize fertility rates decline and participation of women in the labor force increases.

As was discussed in chapter two, studies indicate that in pre-industrial agricultural societies, the relative compatibility of work with childrearing enables women to perform farm work along with child care and housework as all activities take place in the same location. In these societies, a woman's social status is defined by who she marries and by motherhood. Work outside the home is not valued but a great deal of value is placed on a woman's reproductive role. Children in agricultural societies are viewed as an economic asset and source of cheap labor (Caldwell, 1976). Furthermore, parents in agricultural and less economically developed societies draw upon their children to improve their own standard of living, and because preindustrial societies lack a social security safety-net, children are relied upon to support their aging parents. Therefore, both parents often prefer to have many children, preferably sons, to insure that enough children survive to take care of them in their old age. Caldwell calls this the *intergenerational transfer of resources*. Women as well as men support the idea of large families since women are likely to outlive their husbands (this is particularly true in patriarchal societies where men frequently marry women much younger than themselves) and during widowhood they have to depend on their children for support (Cain, 1986; Kandiyoti, 1988, 1996).

As mentioned in chapter two, modernization theorists describe the relationship between economic development and female employment (see Boserup, 1970; Haghighat, 2002; Oppenheimer, 1970; Pampel and Tanaka, 1986)[2] as *curvilinear* rather than *linear*. Women's work declines during the transition from an agricultural to industrial economy, but in theory, it picks up again during the transition from an industrial to a postindustrial economy. In preindustrial societies women are able to combine housework and child care with market work (i.e., petty trade, carpet and basket weaving, small-scale farming). Industrialization and urbanization however divides the home and work spheres and limits women's opportunities to participate in the market. Women continue performing their household responsibilities but there is a decline in their market work. As such, their rate of participation in the labor force declines.

However, based on the data gathered from Western societies, the transition from industrialization to post-industrialization should lead to an upswing in women's employment opportunities and their participation in the workforce. Women's reduced fertility rates, the rise in their education, and the existence of job opportunities in the formal sector of the economy (Jelin, 1977; Nash and Safa, 1976; Semyonov, 1980; Wilensky, 1968), all contribute to create a climate conducive to welcoming women into the workforce.

THE CONNECTION BETWEEN FERTILITY, THE TIMING OF MARRIAGE, AND WOMEN'S SOCIAL STATUS

Fertility and its connection to the timing of marriage have implications for women's social status, the organization of family life, educational attainment, and employment patterns (Mensch et al., 2005). The timing of marriage and its connection to fertility has been verified in demographic studies of different parts of the world, especially in the Western world. One could argue that the practice of women marrying at a young age generally results in a higher fertility rate. Early marriage (often measured by women marrying before age eighteen) is considered an important factor in population growth because it extends the number of years a woman can bear children. Applying this analysis to the MENA region we find the results altered by complex social, political, and cultural influences.

In the MENA region, early age at marriage does not always correspond with high fertility. For example, in 2002, about 60 percent of women under age twenty-five (between the ages of fifteen and nineteen, group I; and twenty and twenty-four, group II) were married in the MENA region. In Egypt (group I: 12 percent, group II: 53 percent) and Turkey (group I: 15 percent, group II: 59 percent) a high percentage of women under age twenty-five were married (table 5.1), and yet these two countries' total fertility rates (TFRs) were not as high as expected—3.5 for Egypt and 2.5 for Turkey (see table 5.1). If women getting married at a young age correlates to families having more children, then Egypt and Turkey should have much higher fertility rates. The inconsistencies in these patterns are an indicator of the complex relationships among fertility patterns, marriage practices, and women's status in MENA societies. In this book I will focus on contradictions in the presumption that women who marry early bear more children and, perhaps more importantly, the problems with applying Western modernization patterns to the MENA region.

Historically, in Europe, marrying at an older age has been associated with economic independence and lower fertility (Hanjal, 1965; Wrigley et al., 1997) and this model has been used to speculate on the trajectory of population growth in the MENA region. Being able to establish an independent living (separate from parents and mainly establishing a separate household) was and still is key to creating a new family for young adults. Frequently, postponing marriage is the only way to assure sufficient resources to establish an independent home.

Table 5.1   Selected reproductive health indicators in the MENA region, 2000–2004

	Women married: 15–19 years old (%)	Women married: 20–24 years old (%)	Total Fertility Rate	Married women 15–49, using any method of contraception (%)	Married women 15–49, using modern contraceptives (%)
Algeria	4	30	2.8	64	50
Bahrain	3	30	2.5	62	31
Egypt	12	53	3.5	56	54
Iran	16	—	2.0	74	56
Iraq	—	—	5.3	—	—
Jordan	8	38	3.6	56	39
Kuwait	5	40	4.2	52	39
Lebanon	—	—	2.4	63	40
Libya	1	12	3.9	45	26
Morocco	10	37	3.3	58	49
Oman	15	58	6.1	24	18
Qatar	4	31	3.9	43	32
Saudi Arabia	7	39	5.7	32	29
Syria	11	42	3.8	47	35
Tunisia	1	14	2.1	63	53
Turkey	15	59	2.5	64	38
United Arab Emirates	8	40	3.5	28	24
Yemen	26	70	7.2	21	10
MENA	12	47	3.3	59	45

MENA: Middle East and North African region.

Source: Mensch et al., 2005: 39; Roudi-Fahimi, 2003: table 1, pp. 4–5; 2002 Women of Our World. Population Reference Bureau, Washington, D.C.

Coincident with postponing marriage, young people postponed having children and thereby shortened their period of fecundity. Historically, this resulted in lower birth rates and eventually contributed to population decline in the West. But fertility rates are not only affected by how young a woman is when she gets married. The cultural norms of a society also proscribe gender relations, including when people marry, who they marry, and how many children they have (Malhotra, 1997). There are other factors that have an influence on fertility, regardless of the timing of marriage, such as increased literacy, employment, and successful family planning programs (these factors are explained in detail throughout the book). In traditional patriarchal societies, women are expected to marry at a young age, often to men much older than themselves. The practice of marrying early most likely (but not always) results in high fertility rates. For example, 73 percent of Omani women and 96 percent of Yemeni women were married by age twenty-four in 2002 (see table 5.1). The TFR for Oman and Yemen are 6.1 and 7.2, respectively, the highest in the region and two of the highest TFRs in the world.[3] However, as we saw in this chapter, other MENA countries (e.g., Egypt and Turkey) with a high rate of marriage among young women did not necessarily have a high fertility rate. Therefore, timing of marriage may or may not have a positive correction with fertility rate in the MENA.

In Arab countries, the trend among females getting married before age twenty has dropped significantly in recent decades. Countries such as Libya confirm this trend—28 percent of women in the thirty–thirty-four category are still not married (Fargues, 2003). Libya is an interesting case that is treated separately in the conclusion to this title (chapter nine). In other Arab countries such as Jordan, Kuwait, Morocco, Syria, and Qatar, on average 10 percent of women are still not married at ages thirty–thirty-four (Rashad and Osman, 2003).

To explain the inconsistent interaction between timing of marriage and fertility, we need to consider the parallel effects of increased education, growth in urbanization, and the unique economic reality facing the younger generation in the MENA region; in other words the aftereffects of modernization.[4]

WHAT DOES ISLAM SAY ABOUT THE PRACTICE OF BIRTH CONTROL?

The conventional belief that Islamic tradition or Islamic family law does not allow the use of contraceptives or permit abortion is without merit and has proven to be adaptable in different countries under different circumstances (Morgan et al., 2002; Musallam, 1983; Nasr, 2000; Omran, 1992; Rispler-Chaim, 1999). Islam condones sexual enjoyment within the context of marriage and particularly encourages all Muslims to marry and avoid celibacy. There is also a general consensus among all schools of Islamic law on the permissibility of family planning and lack of explicit objections to it in *Sharia* (Musallam, 1983; Obermeyer, 1992; Roudi-Fahimi, 1988, 2002).

It is true that reduced fertility is often associated with the higher status of women and a greater access to societal resources. Access to family planning programs often helps reduce fertility, and can increase a woman's autonomy, which in turn encourages her participation in the paid employment sector (considering the availability of job opportunities). The MENA region has made great improvements in providing access to reproductive health services for women except in a few countries such as Yemen, Morocco, and Iraq (table 5.1). Most Muslim countries provide direct access to family planning services (UN Report, World Population Policies, 2003) and most have succeeded in lowering their fertility rates for the past few decades. In fact, most MENA countries have a relatively high rate of contraceptive use (table 5.1). Abortion policies in the region vary from one country to another (table 5.2). While most MENA countries prohibit abortion, countries such as Tunisia and Turkey have implemented liberal policies and the rest fall in the middle by placing some restrictions on abortion but not completely banning its practice.

However, family planning programs are highly politicized and governments play a crucial role in banning or promoting them. For example, the institutionalization of an "ideology of female domesticity" or "housewifization" in Iran after the 1979 revolution encouraged pro-natalist ideology. Modern contraceptive methods were discouraged, abortion was banned, and contraceptive devices were removed from pharmacies and clinics (Moghadam, 1993). Between 1976 and 1986 the population increased by 3.9 percent and the TFR was 5.6, which placed Iran among the fastest growing countries in the region. In 1986 about 50 percent of the population was under the age of fifteen. By the end of the 1980s, the unfavorable effects of population increase were felt on the economy, health care services, the educational system, and the work force. The government, influenced by religious leaders, reconsidered its earlier pro-natalist policies, which resulted in a drastic decline of fertility in Iran within a decade. Where does Iran's fertility stand today? With

Table 5.2 Selected reproductive health indicators and abortion policies in the MENA region, 2000

	Births attended by skilled personnel (both rural and urban; %) (1)	Births conducted in health facilities (both rural and urban; %)	Maternal deaths per 100,000 live births (2)	Total Fertility Rate	Abortion policy Liberal (3)	Some restrictions (4)	Prohibited (5)
Algeria	78	76	140	2.8		X	
Bahrain	98	98	46	2.5		X	
Egypt	61	48	84	3.5			X
Iran	90	88	37	2.0			X
Iraq	54	—	290	5.3			X
Jordan	98	97	41	3.6		X	
Kuwait	98	98	5	4.2		X	
Lebanon	89	88	100	2.4			X
Libya	94	94	75	3.9			X
Morocco	40	37	230	3.3		X	
Oman	91	89	14	6.1			X
Qatar	98	98	10	3.9		X	
Saudi Arabia	91	91	23	5.7		X	
Syria	89	55	65	3.8			X
Tunisia	91	90	70	2.1	X		
Turkey	81	73	130	2.5	X		
United Arab Emirates	99	99	3	3.5			X
Yemen	22	16	350	7.2			X
MENA	70	64	130	3.3			

MENA: Middle East and North African region.

(1): Percentage of births attended by skilled personnel. Skilled personnel include doctors, nurses, and midwives. Data refer to the latest survey year through 2001.

(2): Maternal deaths. The number of deaths (mothers) per 100,000 live births that result from conditions related to pregnancy, delivery, and related complications. The estimates for most less developed countries are taken from 1995 consensus estimates of WHO, UNICEF, and UNFPA. Data from Roudi-Fahimi, 2001, table 1, pp. 4–5; 2002 Women of Our World. Population Reference Bureau. Washington, D.C., pp. 46–59.

(3): Liberal: Permitted on broad socioeconomic grounds or without restriction as to reason, within gestational limits. Certain other restrictions may apply, such as spousal and/or parental consent.

(4) Some restrictions: Permitted on physical or mental health grounds—spousal and/or parental consent required in some countries.

(5) Prohibited: Prohibited or permitted only to save a woman's life.

a TFR of 2, Iran has succeeded in reaching the lowest fertility rate in the Middle East region and has the lowest TFR in the developing world (Larsen, 2001; Roudi-Fahimi, 2002). Three-quarters of married women in Iran use contraception, which is the highest rate among Muslim countries and comparable to many Western nations including the United States. In 2002, the United States' TFR was 2.1 compared with 2.0 for Iran.

The importance of the role of the government in the promotion or dismissal of family planning programs has been influential in the success or failure of family planning programs in MENA countries. Although Islamic law does not prohibit the practice of family planning and does not encourage high fertility, the pro-natalist orientation of Islam is based not on direct injunctions, but indirectly on the political conditions created that are conducive to high fertility (Fagley, 1965; Obermeyer, 1992, 1994). Countries such as Algeria and Iran saw fertility decline dramatically while experiencing the rise and domination of Islamic fundamentalism (Fargues, 2003).

Obermeyer (1994), in studying the impact of Islam on fertility behavior in Iran and Tunisia, concludes that the reproductive behavior in these countries is a function of the government's policy changes rather than the impact of the population's religious beliefs. By addressing economic, social, and cultural barriers through the educational system and the media, governments can play an important role in facilitating the use of health and family planning services in Muslim countries. The governments of Egypt and Iran have played a crucial role in implementing successful family planning programs. The governments consciously use religion to manipulate the population depending on the needs of the economy. In Egypt, for example, religious leaders sent out messages of *fatwas* (religious rulings) in favor of modern contraception. Government health care facilities distribute contraceptive devices and therefore make them available to couples from all levels of economic and social classes.

The success of family planning programs supported by the Iranian government and the cooperation of the religious leaders is progressive in that the sole focus is not on a woman's responsibility for reducing fertility, they also place a great deal of importance on the man's roles in reducing fertility. Larsen (2001) states:

> One of the strengths of Iran's promotion of family planning is the involvement of men. Iran is the only country in the world

that requires both men and women to take a class on modern contraception before receiving a marriage license. And it is the only country in the region with a government-sanctioned condom factory. In the past four years, some 220,000 Iranian men have had a vasectomy. While vasectomies still account for only 3 percent of contraception, compared with female sterilization at 28 percent, men nonetheless are assuming more responsibility for family planning. (P. 2)

On the opposite end of the spectrum, the Yemeni government has made no effort to control and prevent the country's high fertility rate (7.2), high child mortality rate, and high maternal mortality; in fact, they deploy ideologies in the name of Islam to reinforce the rule of high fertility (see table 5.2 for selective reproductive health indicators for Yemen and other MENA countries). Yemen has the least favorable demographic record (high fertility, high mortality, low women's status, low modernization, low women's employment, no participation of women in politics) compared to other MENA countries. A large percentage of Yemeni women believe that Islam does not condone use of contraception.[5] Therefore Yemeni women and men are reluctant to use birth control methods as it is considered "un-Islamic" to do so. Since Yemen has such a poor record on health care, which leads to high mortality rates, a high rate of fertility is necessary to replace the population.[6]

Multilevel analysis and demographic studies comparing Muslim and non-Muslim communities in India, Malaysia, Thailand, and the Philippines ask whether there is a religion-based difference between those communities regarding fertility related decisions—whether or not to have more children, whether or not to use contraception, and so on (Morgan et al., 2002). The study finds that the important variable is not of Muslim versus non-Muslim, but rather of age at first marriage, employment outside the house, and number of years of schooling; a greater level of autonomy (indicator of women's social status) in both types of communities leads to reduced fertility rates (Morgan et al., 2002). The study concluded no religion-based difference between the two groups and their fertility levels and women's decision-making power (again, an indicator of women's status within the household and family). Olmsted (2003), in her study of the MENA countries, examines what she calls the "fertility puzzle." She tests variables such as income, government policies, women's labor force participation, and cultural factors and, like Morgan et al. (2002), finds that female education and age at marriage are among the most significant factors in determining fertility levels. Thus, Islam alone does not affect women's fertility patterns.

WOMEN, JOBS, AND FERTILITY

Women's employment patterns are linked to fertility rates. Studies show that when women have the opportunity to earn their own incomes, they tend to delay marriage and parenthood and hence bear fewer children in their lifetime (Brewster and Rindfuss, 2000). Employment has an effect on fertility in both directions—women may choose not to work if they have children, and for women who are working, it may influence the number of children they choose to have.

Social and cultural changes such as a decline in fertility rates, an increase in age at marriage, and a demand for more educated men and women, all contribute to a larger supply of younger women who are, at least, temporarily freed from family responsibilities (i.e., early marriage, subsequent pregnancies, child care responsibilities, housework) and therefore more available to be employed. Singh (1994), using cross-national data, evaluates the effect of women's contraceptive use and availability, and the use of health services by mothers at birth on fertility, mortality, women's education, and labor force participation in developing countries. She finds that women's educational attainment (measured by school enrollments and/or the number of school years completed) had a restraining effect on fertility and mortality rates. Needless to say, using contraceptives leads to a decline in fertility rates, and the availability of health services to mothers at birth leads to a lower rate of child mortality.

In general, similar to most of the developing world, the majority of Muslim societies face the dilemma of a high fertility rate (but declining) and as a result, high population growth rates. The World Fertility Survey reports that fertility was the highest in the MENA region but currently the region holds the second highest rank in the world. Fertility rate is declining in all regions over recent years except in sub-Saharan Africa. Although the MENA region is experiencing one of the highest population growth rates in the world, it has also made dramatic improvements in reducing fertility in some of its countries such as Iran, Lebanon, and Tunisia. The lingering effect of the previously higher rate of fertility is that they still have a disproportionately large young population to educate, employ, and provide social services for. The economic instability in the region coupled with patriarchal tradition means that women are not the priority of the government and therefore are pushed aside. In sum, despite the declining fertility rates there has been no comparable increase in women's employment as would be projected by the modernization theory.

CHAPTER 6

EDUCATION AND STATUS
OF WOMEN

Many factors influence women's status including fertility, education, employment, and modernization. In this chapter we will specifically examine the effect of formal education on women's status in the MENA. While a person's informal education is obtained through the socialization process (i.e., family, religion), formal education is obtained through schooling in a formal, structured manner. Giddens et al. (2005) state:

> Until the first few decades of the 19th century, most of the world's population had no schooling...But as the industrial economy rapidly expanded, there was a great demand for specializing schooling that could produce an educated, capable work force. As occupations became more differentiated and were increasingly located away from the home, it was impossible for work skills to be passed on directly from parents to children. (P. 476)

Therefore, by formal education we shall limit our considerations to the process of schooling (children attending schools and education being considered as an institution).

In the MENA region, sometimes the effects of women's education deviate from the expectations of the modernization perspective, while at other times we will see that the effects of women's education are rendered ineffective due to the dominant influence of cultural forces. Modernization theory shows a strong relationship between increased access to education and positive changes in women's status. While the MENA region is going through the modernization process, the results do not mirror the West. In the countries of the MENA the strong ties to patriarchal culture and the integration of religion into government complicate the analysis of education and women's status.

Formal education—as an important feature of modernization—emerged in the West in the early decades of the nineteenth century. Schools were established in different parts of Europe and the United States with the goal of providing access to formal education for most children. As the industrial economy expanded, an educated and knowledgeable workforce was needed and providing options for formal education became an important feature of industrializing nations. While preindustrial societies did not have a need for educated individuals with knowledge of abstract subject matters (such as math, science, and literature), industrial and postindustrial knowledge-based economies increasingly needed an educated and literate population.

The advent of formal and mass education in the modern MENA region is closely connected to the influence of the West and the era of colonization. During the nineteenth and early twentieth centuries, children from middle class and elite families would receive religious and language lessons from private tutors or from places called *Maktab* (equivalent to a school but lessons were conducted on a one-on-one basis with a tutor). Overall, access to modern education was restricted to a select few and mainly reserved for the children of the elite—mostly their sons. The colonizers were not keen on educating the masses since the belief was that intellectual development would lead to the colonizer's loss of political influence and control (Abdeljalil, 2004; Said, 1993).

Countries such as Tunisia, Egypt, and Iran made investments in a handful of their elite children by sending them to European countries to learn about the latest technologies and ways of life. This ultimately had the effect of diffusing knowledge about the West when the students returned to their own countries. Furthermore, local schools could have a significant impact on disseminating knowledge about the West. For example, the Polytechnic School of Bardo (modeled after the French *Ecole Polytechnique*), established in Tunisia in the 1830s, was taught and administered by the French and Tunisians educated in France (Abdeljalil, 2004).

In countries such as Iran, schools were available for non-Muslim girls in the 1830s, but political resistance from Islamic clergy prevented the schooling of Muslim girls until the first decade of the twentieth century. Muslim girls were kept illiterate or, in the case of the children of the elite, tutored privately at home. Even though the schools were available, there was limited support from families to send their daughters to school.

The first school in Iran that opened its doors to Muslim girls was established in Tehran in 1899. These schools were attended by daughters of the elite and the progressive middle class Iranian families, whereas non-Muslim girls (middle class Christian, Zoroastrian, Jewish) had been attending the few missionary schools that were available to them for at least seventy-five years prior to 1899 (Nashat, 1983; Shavarini, 2006). Up until the schools opened, daughters of the Muslim elite would often receive some basic education by private tutors in subject matters such as Persian literature, religious studies and French language, and literature. Shavarini's (2006) and Nashat's (1983) description of Iran's history of education for women was representative of the history of women's education in other parts of the MENA region. In many of these countries, especially the ones under direct influence of colonizers—such as Lebanon, Egypt, and Tunisia—bilingualism among elite families became widespread by the late nineteenth century. It became a way to learn about Western cultural practices and technological advancements, and was also a way for the children of the elite to distinguish themselves from others by claiming a higher status and a higher level of literacy and knowledge of the Western cultures.

In different parts of the MENA, political leaders attempted to "modernize" their countries during the first part of the twentieth century by giving women more access to societal resources such as formal education. Under their leadership, Reza Khan in Iran, Ataturk in Turkey, and Habibullah Khan in Afghanistan tried to implement programs to modernize their countries in the 1920s and 1930s. One important aspect of their modernization process was to give women more rights and to allow them to have access to schools for Muslim girls. Mass education for girls was also accompanied by an attempt to de-institutionalize the practice of *hijab*. These leaders had the difficult task of convincing religious authorities that modern secular education did not clash with *Sharia* and furthermore, it would not "contaminate" the minds of young women who were sent abroad to study at European colleges. These leaders saw women's education as one of the main avenues to westernize/modernize their countries, and they also challenged the structure of patriarchal and tribal relations. However, none of the three leaders stayed in power for long and their successors continued to experience resistance from rigid fundamentalist Islamist forces for decades to come.

After World War II and particularly during the 1950s–1970s in the MENA region, there was a dramatic rise in the popularity of educating young women. Girls were integrated into gender-specific school systems throughout most of the MENA. In the 1970s, however, Islamist movements across the MENA mounted strong opposition to giving girls and women access to education and to the presence of women in the workforce. For example, in Iran, during the 1979 Islamic revolution led by Ayatollah Khomeini, women were among the most loyal revolutionary fighters against the Shah's regime. Afterward, they were also among the first to be sent home and deprived of their access to education and employment as soon as Ayatollah Khomeini's regime took power. Eventually, Iranian women and girls recovered some access to educational institutions after the government "Islamicized" education in schools and universities. Women were allowed access as long as the educational institutions followed the strict rules of the Islamists.

In Afghanistan, however, women have always been subject to strict tribal and patriarchal rules. Furthermore, their social status is complicated by a low level of economic development and a high rate of poverty. Their oppression became even more extreme under the U.S. backed Mujahedeen. In the 1970s Islamist resistance groups rallied in Kabul demanding that women be prevented from holding any public office, enforcing the return of the hijab, and ending coeducation in schools.

When the Soviet Union pulled its troops from Afghanistan in 1989 and the Mujahedeen took power, ordering women out of political life was among their first changes. Then, they threatened women and girls to abide by oppressive rules, such as wearing a full *Burgha*. Frequently, families were ordered to pull their daughters out of school. These actions created an even larger gap between boys' and girls' education rates. When the fundamentalist (originally supported by the United States and Pakistan) Taliban regime emerged in 1993, the suppression of women reached its most extreme point in the history of Afghanistan. Women were forbidden to work and forced to leave their jobs and schools. They had to become completely invisible in public life and were even forbidden to be seen outside of their homes. The U.S. government's invasion of Afghanistan, after September 11, 2001, toppled the Taliban and allowed women back in public spaces. Eventually some girls returned to school. However, Afghanis, especially Afghani women, continue to suffer from centuries of poverty and an absence of economic development. Their oppression is still visible in their low social status and particularly in their high levels of illiteracy.

MODERNIZATION AND EDUCATION

Modernization theorists argue that formal education plays a central role in modern societies,[1] and credentialism (acquiring education with degrees and diplomas) becomes an important stepping stone for job opportunities, access to societal resources, and a successful life (Collins, 1979). Policymakers also argue that an educated society is a more productive and affluent one, especially in regions such as the MENA where poverty is not as deep as in other developing regions (Van Eeghen and Soman, 1997). They also acknowledge that improving education and employment opportunities are more helpful to improving women's lives than other factors that require deeper cultural intervention (Castro Martin, 1995; Dasgupta, 1995). For example, studies show that educated women use contraceptives significantly more frequently than illiterate women.

The UN Population Fund (2002) reports that countries that have made social investments in education, health, and reproductive services experience faster economic improvement and slower population growth. Roudi and Moghadam (2003) list the benefits of female education on women's empowerment and gender equality:

- As female education rises, fertility, population growth, and infant and child mortality fall and family health improves.
- Increases in girls' secondary school enrollment are associated with increases in women's participation in the labor force and their contributions to household and national income.
- Women's increased earning capacity, in turn, has a positive effect on child nutrition.
- Children—especially daughters—of educated mothers are more likely to be enrolled in school and to have higher levels of educational attainment.
- Educated women are more politically active and better informed about their legal rights and how to exercise them. (P. 4)

EDUCATION AND FERTILITY

Education has been shown to affect a wide range of behaviors such as the postponement and timing of marriage, the number of children conceived, and the participation of women in the labor force (Bongaarts refers to education as one of the proximate determinants[2] of fertility). The relationship between education and fertility has been closely studied and suggests that women's education does not necessarily produce similar results in every society but is "conditioned by socioeconomic development, social structure, and cultural context, as well as by a society's stage in the fertility transition" (Castro Martin, 1995: 199). Graff (1979) argues that education has a more substantial impact on the "psychological modernity" of people in societies that are experiencing industrialization—that, in modernizing societies, there is a connection between increased education and reduced fertility. He applies psychological modernity to men's and women's acceptance of family limitations, control of one's fertility, and the subsequent decline in population growth. Ali (2002), in his ethnographic study of urban and rural communities in Egypt, came to the same conclusion—that people's more modern attitudes and thinking processes are the main reason they take advantage of family planning services that lowers their fertility rate. Freedman (1995) finds a consistent correlation between education and literacy and demographic outcomes such as fertility rates with the exception of anomalous cases such as Bangladesh (a majority Muslim nation and one of the most populous Muslim countries). Bangladesh still struggles with a low level of female literacy, but through effective family planning programs, the country had succeeded in lowering its fertility rate despite its still high mortality rate. It is estimated that 45 percent of Bangladeshi couples use contraceptives (Freedman 1995). Therefore, fertility rate has been lowered in the context of female illiteracy rate. Bangladesh is considered an exceptional case but the literature shows a strong case for the education-low fertility nexus.

When women in the upper educational range are compared with women in the lower range across one society, fertility is substantially lower among better educated women (Castro Martin and Juarez, 1995; Weinberger et al., 1989). Castro Martin (1995: 190) reports on the World Fertility Survey (WFS) and Demographic Health Survey (DHS) results and concludes that, in general, societies with limited literacy and limited schooling have high fertility rates, but as societies advance and education becomes more available fertility rates start to drop. In most societies, more educated women use modern contraception more frequently than uneducated women:

> [In Latin America] women with no formal schooling have, on average, six to seven children, whereas highly educated women have fertility levels analogous to those found in the developed world, in the range of two to three children...[In the sub-Saharan African region] the association between female education and fertility appears weakest...prior studies have attributed this atypical pattern to the dominance of physiological factors in a context of natural fertility. In the absence of conscious birth control, education has the potential of increasing fertility as a result of reduced breastfeeding and postpartum abstinence. (Ibid.)

Gender disparity in education is an ongoing problem in many parts of the developing world although an overwhelming majority of the countries in the MENA have narrowed gender gaps in literacy.[3] In Iran and Kuwait, for example, female college enrollments oftentimes have exceeded male enrollments. The gender gap in primary school level has narrowed or disappeared in almost all parts of the world but is still pronounced at the secondary school and tertiary level (UN Population Fund, 2002). Promotion and expansion of formal education has been closely linked to ideals of democracy and an effective strategy to reduce poverty in developing societies. The overall trend seems to indicate that the gender gap in schooling is slowly closing, but there is still much progress to be made.

The data in table 6.1 compares illiteracy rates between men and women. The data are listed for each gender by individual country in MENA, different world regions, age group, and time period. Column two compares illiteracy rates for men and women, fifteen years of age and older in 2000. This group is a snapshot of the entire adult population of each country/ region and serves as a baseline for a comparison of the changes that took effect over four years from 2000 to 2004. The second group (column three) shows the illiteracy rates of men and women, ages fifteen–twenty-four years, and during the period of 2000–2004. By contrasting the first and second groups, we can determine the rate and direction of change in illiteracy, which serves as an indicator of the change in education. By restricting the second group to the fifteen–twenty-four age group, we can focus on progress made by those most likely to be in or having just completed the education process, that is, the education level of the entire population (group 1) compared to the education of the younger generation of fifteen–twenty-four-year-olds.

Examining this table, we can draw several conclusions:

- Examining countries making up the MENA, we see that from group 1, there is an increase in literacy in the case of every country. Considering the MENA region as a whole, the overall illiteracy rate among women shows a reduction in the 2000–2004 period as compared to the 2000 period. The world illiteracy rate among women (last line in the table) shows the same global reduction in the 2000–2004 periods as compared to the 2000 period.

Table 6.1 Selected literacy indicators in the MENA region

Country	Illiterate (15 years or older; in %), 2000		Illiterate (ages 15–24; in %), 2000/2004		Literate women as % of literate men (ages 15–24), 2000–2004
	Female	Male	Female	Male	
Algeria	43	24	16	7	91
Bahrain	17	9	1	2	101
Egypt	56	33	37	24	85
Iran	31	17	9	4	95
Iraq	77	45	71	41	49
Jordan	16	5	1	1	100
Kuwait	20	16	7	8	102
Lebanon	20	8	7	3	96
Libya	32	9	7	0.05	94
Morocco	64	38	42	24	79
Oman	38	20	4	0.5	98
Qatar	17	20	3	7	102
Saudi Arabia	33	17	10	5	96
Syria	40	12	21	5	96
Tunisia	39	19	11	3	93
Turkey	24	7	6	1	95
United Arab Emirates	21	25	6	13	108
Yemen	75	33	54	17	60
Region					
MENA	42	22	23	11	—
Africa	48	30	31	19	—
Latin America/ Caribbean	14	11	4	5	—
North America	—	—	—	—	—
More developed	—	—	—	—	—
Less developed	34	19	19	12	92
World	31	17	18	11	92

MENA: Middle East and North African region.

Sources: Women of Our World. 2005. *Population Reference Bureau*, Washington, D.C.; 2005 World Population Data Sheet. *Population Reference Bureau*, Washington, D.C.; United Nations Development Programme (UNDP), *Human Development Report* 2003. New York: UNDP, 2003; Roudi-Fahimi and Moghadam (2003).

- Table 6.1 also allows us to rank the MENA region among different regions of the world. The comparison ranks reduction in female illiteracy in the MENA as third, behind Latin America and less-developed category of countries. MENA is ahead of African region only in reducing female illiteracy rate.

- Comparing the world to the category of less-developed nations, the change is almost the same. The MENA region shows a reduction of 45 percent while less-developed nations collectively show a 44 percent reduction in female illiteracy rate.

PATTERNS OF EDUCATION IN THE MENA REGION

Until the late 1970s, the MENA region had one of the highest illiteracy rates in the world compared with other less-developed nations. Three decades later, 42 percent of women (age fifteen or more) and 22 percent of men (age fifteen or more) were illiterate in the region compared with 34 percent of women and 19 percent of men in other less-developed nations (table 6.1). A few countries report 60 percent or more of their female population over age fifteen being illiterate (Morocco, 64 percent; Yemen, 75 percent; Iraq 77 percent), while a female illiteracy rate of 20 percent or less is reported for Bahrain, Jordan, Kuwait, Lebanon, and Qatar.

In 2000–2004, the younger generation of women and men (between ages fifteen–twenty-four) in both the MENA region and the less-developed countries had a lower percentage of illiterates among their population (23 percent of women and 11 percent of men in the MENA region and 19 percent of women and 12 percent of men in less-developed countries). The reduction in illiteracy among the younger generation is an indication that these countries' governments are providing better access to education, and perhaps also an indication that there is a societal shift in thinking about the relevance of education for women. Almost all the countries in the MENA region report that nearly all of their children (both boys and girls) are enrolled in primary school (table 6.2). It was seen that 91 percent of girls and 100 percent of boys were enrolled in primary school in year 2000. Omani and Yemeni girls still fall behind their counterparts (71 and 61 percent, respectively) but other countries show near perfect statistics for male and female primary school enrollment.

Roughly half of the countries in the MENA countries have succeeded in significantly reducing illiteracy among their younger generations of women and men (nine of the eighteen countries within the MENA region report illiteracy rates of less than 10 percent for both boys and girls aged fifteen–twenty-four years).

Table 6.2 Selected education indicators in the MENA region

| Country | % Enrolled in primary school, 2000 | | % Enrolled in Secondary School | | | | | | Women as share of university enrollment (%), 2000 | Public education as share of total government expenditure (%) |
| | | | 1985 | | 1993–1997 | | 2000/2003 | | | |
	Female	Male	Female	Male	Female	Male	Female	Male		
Algeria	107	116	44	59	62	65	74	69	—	16
Bahrain	103	103	97	98	98	91	99	91	60	12
Egypt	96	103	50	72	73	83	85	91	—	15
Iran	85	88	36	54	73	81	75	79	47	18
Iraq	91	111	39	68	32	51	29	47	34	—
Jordan	101	101	—	—	—	—	87	86	51	20
Kuwait	95	93	87	95	66	64	88	83	68	14
Lebanon	97	101	60	61	84	78	81	74	52	8
Libya	117	115	57	61	—	—	108	102	48	—
Morocco	88	101	28	42	34	44	36	45	44	25
Oman	71	74	18	35	79	80	78	79	58	16
Qatar	104	105	86	79	66	68	93	88	73	—
Saudi Arabia	—	—	31	48	57	65	65	73	56	23
Syria	105	113	48	68	40	45	42	47	—	14
Tunisia	115	120	32	46	63	66	81	78	48	20
Turkey	96	105	30	52	48	68	66	86	41	15
United Arab Emirates	99	99	55	55	82	77	82	77	—	20
Yemen	61	96	—	—	14	53	27	65	21	22

Continued

Table 6.2 Continued

Country	% Enrolled in primary school, 2000		% Enrolled in Secondary School						Women as share of university enrollment (%), 2000	Public education as share of total government expenditure (%)
			1985		1993–1997		2000/2003			
	Female	Male	Female	Male	Female	Male	Female	Male		
Region										
MENA	91	100	—	—	50	60	62	71	—	—
World	—	—	43	54	55	63	62	67	—	—
Africa	—	—	23	33	32	38	36	41	—	—
Latin America/ Caribbean	—	—	—	—	—	—	90	83	—	—
North America	—	—	97	97	98	99	93	95	—	—
More developed	—	—	94	93	102	99	103	101	—	—
Less developed	—	—	31, 44	44	47	57	55	61	—	—

MENA: Middle East and North African region.

Sources: Roudi-Fahimi and Moghadam (2003); *Women of Our World.* 2005. *Population Reference Bureau,* Washington, D.C.; 2005 World Population Data Sheet. *Population Reference Bureau.* Washington, D.C.; United Nations Development Programme (UNDP), *Human Development Report* 2003.

Those countries are Bahrain, Iran, Jordan, Kuwait, Lebanon, Libya, Oman, Qatar, and Turkey. Iraq, Yemen, Morocco, and Egypt still have a significant population of women in the fifteen–twenty-four age bracket (ranging from 71 percent in Iraq to 37 in Egypt) who are illiterate (table 6.1). The illiteracy rate among women over fifteen is still high in several other countries in the MENA where women are roughly twice as likely as men to be illiterate in that age group (Olmsted, 2005; UNIFEM, 2004).

PRIMARY, SECONDARY, AND TERTIARY EDUCATION

As stated earlier, in many of the MENA countries the gender gap in providing education is closing. Most children in the region are enrolled in primary school (91 percent of girls and 100 percent boys). But not all countries have been able to provide equal access to secondary school enrollment. Only 62 percent of girls and 71 percent of boys were enrolled in secondary school. Countries such as Libya and Bahrain have an impressive 91–108 percent[4] rate for secondary school enrollment while Syria, Morocco, and Yemen show rates of 42, 36, and 27 percent, respectively, for female enrollment in secondary school respectively.

However, in the two decades between 1980 and early-to-mid-2000, many countries experienced a dramatic jump in the enrollment of both male and female students in secondary school (see table 6.3). For example, in 1985, 57 percent of women in Libya were enrolled in secondary school compared with 108 percent in year 2000. Oman and Tunisia provide other great examples; only 18 percent of girls in Oman and 32 percent in Tunisia were enrolled in secondary school in 1985. By the year 2000, 78 and 81 percent of girls were enrolled in Oman and Tunisia, respectively. Table 6.3 illustrates the percentage of change in secondary school enrollment in the MENA region. Almost all countries have improved male and female secondary schooling since 1985. There are some fluctuations for countries such as Syria and Lebanon but the decline is not consistent. The one consistent decline for secondary school enrollment, for both boys and girl, is in Iraq. Iraq has failed to improve secondary school enrollment for boys and girls since 1985 (the enrollment has decreased). The reason for this decline could be due

Table 6.3 Percentage change in secondary school enrollment in the MENA region, between 1985 and 1993–1997 and 1993–1997 and 2000–2003

Country	Females: change in secondary school enrollment, between 1985 and 1993–1997 (in %)	Males: change in secondary school enrollment, between 1985 and 1993–1997 (in %)	Females: change in secondary school enrollment, from 1993–1997 to 2000–2003 (in %)	Males: change in secondary school enrollment, from 1993–1997 to 2000–2003 (in %)
Algeria	41	11	20	6
Bahrain	1	–7	1	0
Egypt	46	15	16	10
Iran	103	50	3	–2.5
Iraq	–18	–25	–9	–8
Jordan	—	—	—	—
Kuwait	–24	–33	33	30
Lebanon	40	28	–4	–5
Libya	—	—	6	—
Morocco	21	5	–1	2
Oman	339	129	41	–1
Qatar	–23	–14	14	29
Saudi Arabia	84	35	5	12
Syria	–17	–34	29	4
Tunisia	97	44	38	18
Turkey	60	31	0	27
United Arab Emirates	49	40	93	0
Yemen	—	—	—	23

MENA: Middle East and North African region.

Sources: Roudi-Fahimi and Moghadam (2003); Women of Our World. 2005. *Population Reference Bureau*, Washington, D.C.; 2005 World Population Data Sheet. *Population Reference Bureau*. Washington, D.C.; United Nations Development Programme (UNDP), Human *Development Report* 2003.

to its depressed economy and continuous political conflicts and wars during the past two decades.

Women's share of university enrollment is impressive in some of the Arab Gulf countries (Saudi Arabia, 56 percent; Oman, 58 percent; Bahrain, 60 percent; Kuwait, 68 percent; and Qatar, 73 percent) and low for Yemen and Iraq (20 and 34 percent, respectively). In countries where women make up the majority of the university population it is because men seek greater social status by leaving the country to attend foreign universities (Roudi-Fahimi and Moghadam, 2003). Families with the financial resources prefer to send their sons to European and American universities not only to learn the latest technology, but also to increase their social status with the foreign degree. Daughters, however, are still kept close to the family home and so are more likely to populate the local universities. The number of sons going overseas for university is enough, in the wealthy states, to skew the data comparing local university attendance by gender.

In general, governments in MENA countries spend a high percentage of their GDP on education expenditures (Sarbib, 2002). As noted earlier, statistics reflect the region's improvement in literacy rates during the past three decades—all boys and over 90 percent of girls have been enrolled in elementary schools. Additionally, 62 percent of girls and 71 percent of boys were reported to be enrolled in secondary school in the year 2000 (table 6.2).

EDUCATION AND EMPLOYMENT

According to modernization theory, education is expected to pull more women into the labor force, but statistics show otherwise. About 27 percent of women in the MENA region are reported to be employed, which is considered to be the lowest rate compared with other regions (Africa, Asia, Europe, Latin American, and North America). In spite of higher achievements in female education rates, the female unemployment rate is still disproportionately high relative to men; within the MENA region, the gulf monarchies (or GCC) report having the lowest rate of women's employment.[5] For many reasons, these countries' female labor force participation rates are inflated by an unusually large number of foreign female workers. (This argument will be explored in further detail in chapter eight.)

A society's investment in education is generally assumed to pay off in the creation of more jobs (mainly in the nonagricultural sector) and better educated individuals in the workforce. For a society to receive returns on its investments on education, it needs to build a skilled and flexible labor force. Contrary to expectations, the MENA region's substantial investment in education has not been paying off as expected. There is little evidence that education has contributed to economic growth in the region (Nabli, 2002). The Arab Human Development Report (2002) indicates that one in five Arabs still live on less than $2 a day. Over the past twenty years, growth in income per person at an annual rate of 0.5 percent was lower than anywhere else in the world except in sub-Saharan Africa. Stagnant economic growth together with a fast-growing population has contributed to high unemployment. About twelve million people, or 15 percent of the labor force, are already unemployed in the Arab world (Arab Human Development Report, 2002). Therefore, despite their great improvements in education, the unemployment rate especially among the educated is high, in some cases an astounding 15–20 percent.

THE CONNECTION BETWEEN EDUCATION, WOMEN'S IMPROVED SOCIAL STATUS, AND PAID EMPLOYMENT—A PARADOX

Historically modernization has occurred in conjunction with industrialization; a successful process of growth and diversification due to a growing domestic economy through the export of goods and services. In the MENA region we see modernization has been accompanied with economic stagnation and regional political conflicts. The result of modernization is therefore different than what is expected.[6]

The high rate of women's access to secondary and higher education in most of the MENA region is impressive although much improvement is still needed. According to modernization theorists and based on the experience of many Western societies, more educated women are more empowered women. They claim that as educational access for women improves, it creates more favorable conditions for women to enter the labor force. Therefore the number of women working increases with a higher degree of industrialization (Durand, 1975). Social and cultural changes such as marriage at a later age, declining fertility rates, and a demand for a more educated labor force, all contribute to a larger supply of female workers. The demand for a more educated labor force in modernizing societies is generally assumed to work in women's favor since modernization also increases women's access to better jobs.

And yet, as women's education level has increased in the MENA region, their labor force participation has not increased as expected. As of year 2000, women's formal employment in the MENA region was as low as 27 percent. Lattouf (2004) attributes this low rate—despite their improved educational attainment—to women's lack of improved social status. For example, she examines women's social status in modern Lebanon and identifies several factors contributing to their lack of economic success despite their high level of education. She argues that economic stagnation and regional political problems led the government to run campaigns to legitimize discrimination against women and force women to operate within the traditional cultural framework— in the home and with limited social power.

Lattouf (2004) states that:

- Despite low rates of return on education for women in terms of employment income, families educate their daughters with the idea of finding them more suitable husbands. A woman through higher level of education and choice of a husband can achieve a higher social and financial status (p. 17). Education is not a stepping stone to greater autonomy for women, but rather a way to achieve a higher level of social status, but still as a dependant.
- Advocating women's rights is connected directly with the West and national disloyalty. Women and men are bombarded by popular messages in the regional media that stress traditional gender roles, where it is emphasized that women's primary roles are housewife and mother. Her employment is portrayed as unimportant to her and her family despite her level of educational achievement.
- Education and employment changes initiated at the institutional level will work only if they are administered along with socialization tactics to change attitudes and behaviors of people on a personal level.

A similar study by Mitra Shavarini (2006) reveals similar constraints on women in Iranian society. A notable 62 percent of women compared with 38 percent of men passed the national college entrance examination called *Konkur* in 2003, indicating that a larger percentage of women are applying to college than men. Closing the educational gender gap and surpassing men in attending and receiving post-secondary degrees is an achievement for Iranian women. However, the advances in educational attainment do not correlate to an increase of women in the workforce or an up-tick in social status except by extension through a good marriage.

In her study of female college students, Shavarini describes the experiences of women in present day Iranian institutions of higher education and the challenges female students face in their everyday life. Shavarini tries to answer two main questions in her ethnographic study: "1) what role does higher education plays in the lives of Iranian women? and 2) what are the experiences of Iranian women at these institutions?" (p. 189). Shavarini's posits that women's ability to gain access to higher education at an increasing rate is explained in part by the "Islamic packaging" of higher education. She states that women's access to colleges "reveals that college has become the only viable institution through which young Iranian women can alter their public role and status." (p. 193). Here is a quote from one of her respondents: "The only right women find that is granted to them and is encouraged is the right to an education...In today's Iranian society, women are considered 'second-class citizens.' They have no rights; no place in society, there is a place for women's rights. Going to the university has become the only thing that we are allowed to do" (p. 199).

Many of the women interviewed by Shavarini had the full support of their families to obtain a higher education. However, the support and promotion of a college experience for women by their families was often mentioned as a way to improve their daughter's chances of finding a suitable husband of similar or higher social status. Many of these women were aware they were facing societal discrimination when it came to finding jobs even with their higher education degrees. The discrimination is a consequence of living in an economically depressed country such as Iran, with a high inflation rate and a high rate of unemployment. Men are given priority in access to jobs and therefore highly qualified women with college degrees are unable to find suitable employment. Discrimination against women is partially an expedient response to the faltering economy and has its roots in history and culture. For the most part, in a strongly patriarchal society men are the breadwinners, and many women are dependent on the male members of their family including father, brother, uncle, husband, and son. From a political standpoint, it makes sense to ensure that men are not facing competition from women for jobs especially where there is a scarcity of work. The deep historical roots of the patriarchal social structure and support from religion for this system lead to women's discrimination in the labor force, which is further compounded by economic stagnation, political conflicts, and global events. The rate at which the new jobs are created lags behind the growth of the number of young people entering the job market. The MENA region suffers from an unusually high rate of unemployment not only for women but for men as well. In 2006 the unemployment rate for men and women averaged 10 and 17 percent, respectively (ILO, 2007). Unemployment rate is further complicated by age; the younger generation of men and women are experiencing even higher unemployment rate in the MENA region than the older age groups. Roudi-Fahimi and Kent (2007) express this concern:

> While less than 15 percent of young men and women were unemployed worldwide, the ILO estimated that just over 20 percent of young men and just over 30 percent of young women in MENA were unemployed in 2005. The situation is particularly dire for members of MENA's youth bulge in some countries. More than 40 percent of Algeria's young men and women were unemployed in 2005, which may be why so many Algerians are emigrating [*sic*] to Europe and elsewhere in search of jobs. Between 21 percent and 31 percent of young men were unemployed in Tunisia, Jordan, Saudi Arabia, and several other MENA countries, along with between 29 percent and 50 percent of young women. Qatar, with a labor force dominated by foreign male workers, has relatively low unemployment for young men, but high unemployment for young women. (P. 17)

To illustrate the severity of the low status of women despite their high educational attainment, Shavarini (2006) describes the experience of a female engineering student in the highly competitive Tehran Polytechnic Institute. The female student expresses disappointment and a degree of anger with the discrimination she experiences each day and the lack of prospects for her future:

> My battle starts the minute I walk out of my home each morning. As I am waiting to catch a ride, I endure honks and lurid comments by passing male motorists; during the ride I am made offers of *sigha* [temporary marriage]. At the university gate, I am stopped and told that my makeup and *hijab* are important and in class my comments are dismissed or discredited by my male peers and male professors as "emotional female viewpoints." Do I think I will find a job after I graduate? What man in this society is going to take me, take us [women], seriously enough to hire us? (P. 206)

There is no doubt that the fact that these women have access to higher education is a monumental improvement in their educational status. On the other hand, if their status is not improved on a societal level, their higher education credentials will not help them to get far in the job market. As Shirin Ebadi, the Iranian human rights lawyer, activist, and the winner of the 2003 Nobel Peace Prize, concluded, "higher education is paradoxical: it both limits and expands women's possibilities in Iran" (Shavarini 2006: 190).

CHAPTER 7

WORK: DEFINITION AND PATTERNS

The word "work" generally makes people think of engaging in physical and/or mental tasks in exchange for salaries or wages. Although some of us might be lucky enough to hold jobs that are intellectually and emotionally rewarding, many view their jobs as drudgery; a set of tasks that need to be done to get paid.[1] Sociologists, on the other hand, study work and its complex connection to other social institutions. The definition of work and where it takes place changes as societies change. Modernization (discussed in detail in chapter two) describes the process of transition as a society completes one stage of development and enters another. This evolution begins with the society in the preindustrial agriculture stage, it then moves into an industrialized, urbanized stage, and later on to the postindustrial stage. During each transition, change occurs in different aspects of the society including changes in the demographic characteristics of the society; occupational structure, educational opportunities, mortality and fertility patterns. Once societies enter the process of modernization, it is expected that the mortality rate will decline, the fertility rate will drop and education opportunities for both men and women will increase. Changes such as these can bring more opportunities and comfort to women's lives, especially when they are coupled with reduced fertility and reduced household responsibilities. Interestingly, women's participation in the workforce declines during the early transitional stages (from preindustrial agriculture to industrial manufacturing economy) and picks up momentum when the society enters the postindustrial service economy stage.[2] As the formal labor market grows during the early stages and agricultural sector jobs decline, more women leave agricultural work. However, the absence of jobs for women in the early manufacturing economy (explained in detail in the next paragraph) leads to an overall decline in women's employment (Anker and Hein, 1986; Boserup, 1970; Oakley, 1974; Ryan, 1975; Tilly and Scott, 1978). Later on, with job growth in the service and white-collar occupations and continued lower fertility and mortality, women's labor force participation increases again (Evans and Timberlake, 1980; Kentor, 1981; Semyonov, 1980). As discussed in chapter two, the transition from a preindustrial agriculture economy to an early industrial urbanized economy, and later to postindustrial economy, is explained as having a U-shaped effect on women's work (Boserup, 1970; Haghighat, 2002; Oppenheimer, 1970; Pampel and Tanaka, 1986).

Thus, when women's employment declines during the transitional stage—from a preindustrial agricultural economy to an industrial one—changes are also taking place with respect to their households and family responsibilities. In preindustrial societies women are able to combine housework and child care with market work (i.e., petty trade, carpet and basket weaving, small-scale farming). Industrialization and urbanization divide the home and work spheres (work is done in an urban setting removed from the domestic residence). Because the domestic responsibilities remain the primary responsibilities of women, the physical separation of work life and home life limit women's opportunities to participate in the market. Therefore, their rate of participation in the labor force declines (Anker and Hein, 1986). Table 7.1 illustrates the changes in modernizing societies experiencing different stages of modernization with respect to changes in demographic characteristics and their effect on women's work.

Overall, work and home were most likely in the same place in preindustrial, farm societies. But as societies become modernized, urbanized, and industrialized work moves to a new locale. Work and home become two distinct domains and are physically separated from each other. Work is less connected to family and home and more connected to institutions of labor, and a worker's first

Table 7.1 Demographic transition of societies based on the level of modernization

	Preindustrial	Industrial	Postindustrial
Level of urbanization	Least urbanized, mostly rural	Development and expansion of cities, more urbanized but still heavily rural	Mostly urbanized, low level of farming communities
Main industry (where most jobs are located)	Agriculture, farming	Manufacturing, production	Service, knowledge/ information technologH
Demographic characteristics	high fertility, high mortality, low population growth due to high fertility and high mortality	Declining fertility, declining mortality (mortality drops sharply and faster than fertility rate), population growth due to drop in mortality rate and still high or declining fertility rate	Low fertility, low mortality, high level of male and female education, low population growth due to low fertility and low mortality
Female work characteristics	Relatively high level of female labor force participation, mainly agricultural work (farming, petty trade, etc.)	Low level of female labor force participation	Increase in female work—mainly in the service sector

responsibility is to the employer, which may necessitate migration from the rural home to living in the city. While occupations and jobs are relatively simple in preindustrial societies, modernization creates a complex division of labor with more interdependency on specialized labor. Giddens et al. (2005) state:

> The contrast in the division of labor between traditional and modern societies is truly extraordinary. Even in the largest traditional societies, there usually existed no more than 20 to 30 major craft trades, together with such specialized pursuits as merchant, soldier,

and priest. In a modern industrial system, there are literally thousands of distinct occupations. The U.S. Census Bureau lists some 20,000 distinct jobs in the American economy. (P. 416)

Hughes et al. (1999) identify the characteristics of work in modernized societies as follows:

- The separation of work and home results in the separation of leisure and work.
- A hierarchy of authority, as part of the complex organizational structures, takes over the management of work activities. Individuals become a small part of big organizations where they lose the power over their production of goods and services.
- The economic institution becomes the main focus of people's lives and wellbeing, and other institutions (i.e. family, education) serve to accommodate its survival and success. (P. 313)

Examining labor force statistics, as table 7.2 indicates, female labor force participation is relatively low in the MENA region and ranges from 13 percent of the total labor force in UAE to 33 percent of the total labor force in Iran. Bahrain (19 percent), Oman (16 percent), Qatar (14 percent), Saudi Arabia (15 percent), UAE (13 percent), five of the six Gulf Corporation Council (GCC) countries excluding Kuwait (25 percent), show the lowest share of female employment. The Kuwaiti government has managed to create jobs and include women in their labor force. Women are heavily employed in government positions (clerical, teaching, nursing). Over 90 percent of the Kuwaiti female labor force is employed in the public sector. Although Kuwait still uses a large number of guest workers as part of its labor force, other GCC countries are even heavier users of guest workers. The impact of guest workers on employment statistics will be explained in detail in the following chapter.

PAID AND UNPAID WORK AND EMPLOYMENT STATISTICS

Being employed often means being paid for the job that one performs. There is, however, a great deal of work that people perform that is unpaid. For example, the demanding and time-consuming tasks of family care and domestic work,

Table 7.2   Selected indicators of work, 2000–2004

Country	Women's paid work in non-agricultural sector	Women's paid work in agricultural sector	Estimated earned income (PPP US$), 2001		Income disparity between men and women* (in %)
			Female	Male	
Algeria	14.2	—	2,784	9,329	30
Bahrain	—	—	7,578	22,305	34
Egypt	20.3	20.8	1,970	5,075	39
Iran	—	—	2,599	9,301	28
Iraq	—	—	—	—	—
Jordan	21.9	—	1,771	5,800	31
Kuwait	19.7	—	8,605	25,333	34
Lebanon	—	—	1,963	6,472	30
Libya	—	—	—	—	—
Morocco	25.8	19.6	2,057	5,139	40
Oman	25.2	19.1	3,919	17,960	22
Qatar	—	—	—	—	—
Saudi Arabia	14.0	1.8	4,222	21,141	20
Syria	18.4	35.3	1,423	5,109	27
Tunisia	—	—	3,377	9,359	36
Turkey	20.6	48.9	3,717	8,023	46
United Arab Emirates	12.7	0.1	6,041	28,223	21
Yemen	5.8	—	365	1,201	30
High income countries					
Norway	—	—	23,317	36,043	65
Sweden	—	—	19,636	28,817	68
United States	—	—	26,389	45,540	58

* Income disparity is calculated as (female income/male income) * 100.

Sources: 2005 World Development Indicators, Women in Development, table 1.5; Human Development Report 2003, Table 22, Gender-related development; The World Bank Group, GenderStats, Database of Gender Statistics, http://devdata.worldbank.org/genderstats/genderRpt.asp?rpt=profile&cty=BHR,Bahrain&hm=home. Retrieved on August 30, 2007.

primarily carried out by women, are often unpaid. Many societies do not have a formal social service system and women often perform the roles associated with family maintenance such as caring for children, the elderly, and the sick. Therefore household work that is performed outside of the formal economy is for the maintenance, well-being, and support of households and families and is not for exchange on the paid market (Dubeck and Dunn, 2002: 1). Frequently it is not counted in government statistics as "productive work" because it is unpaid. However, the importance of women's work relative to family maintenance should not be underestimated (Donahoe, 1999: 546). Studies in both the developed world (Tienda and Rajman, 1997) and the developing world (Birdsall and McGreevey, 1983; Bruce and Dwyer, 1988; Hoodfar, 1996) reflect on the crucial contribution of women's unpaid work for a family's maintenance and well-being. It should be noted that shifting women's work from the home to the workforce would create a large burden on the government to provide for the sudden loss of domestic services traditionally provided by women: child care, elderly care, and medical attention. The burden is on the government to create jobs for women to enter the workforce while simultaneously providing the family support services that women have traditionally been providing as an unpaid work.

In addition to unpaid housework and child care, women (and oftentimes children) frequently work without pay in a market-oriented establishment or activity that is owned by a relative. The World Bank publishes some data for a limited number of South Asian and Middle Eastern countries on unpaid family workers. There is a gap that exists between men and women's unpaid family work; women are far more likely than men to fall into the category of unpaid family workers. It is estimated that 63 percent of women in Bangladesh are unpaid family workers compared with only 10 percent of males. In Pakistan and Turkey about 50 percent of women were reported as unpaid family workers compared with 17 and 10 percent of men in Pakistan and Turkey, respectively (World Development Indicators, 2005).

Ultimately, despite the significant percentage of women working and contributing to the local economy their contribution is rarely counted in formal employment statistics.

WORK AND THE ROLE OF THE GOVERNMENT—WELFARE STATE TYPOLOGY

Governments play a crucial role in providing work opportunities for their citizens by facilitating labor force participation;

offering incentives, and removing obstacles for employment. But, societies also have rules and norms with respect to men's and women's roles. For example, a study of attitudes toward women's paid work in Germany, Great Britain, and the United States indicates both men and women in these societies approve of women working, but there was a substantial consensus among respondents for a primary familial role for women, especially with young children present (Alwin et al., 1992: 13). The authors also conclude that "attitudes favoring the labor force involvement of women are associated with gender, labor force experience, schooling, and birth cohort. Inter-country differences can in part be explained by normative differences in labor force participation rates of women and perceptions of the suitability of child care resources."

Esping-Anderson (1990), in her study of various industrialized nations, lists different modes of government regimes and the type of services/programs they provide for their citizens, which in turn could encourage or suppress women's participation in the workforce. She examines the differences in terms of each country's employment structure, power structure, and social services provided by the government. Her typology is as follows:

1. *Liberal welfare regime* (i.e., United States, Canada, Australia, and United Kingdom): In these countries the market economy is mainly in charge of providing goods and services. The state will interfere only to prevent unfair competition, monopolies, or if the market fails. In these types of countries, government support systems are limited. Low income groups benefit somewhat from government services but other social classes are not provided with many government's subsidized social services. For example, in the United States, day care services are not provided or paid for by the government. Maternity—paid or unpaid—leave is not mandatory. Often times, women are given desirable job opportunities, similar to men, but there is little or no support for working mothers. The employers might provide day care and other incentives for their employees but these decisions are left to the discretion of the employer.

2. *Conservative welfare regime* (i.e., Germany, Belgium, the Netherlands): These conservative welfare regimes are based on the ideology that married women do not necessarily need to be employed. In fact, the lack of paid employment for women could "preserve the family and maintain existing gender and class differentials" (Bianchi et al., 1999: 8). For married women with children, both social service policy—such as health and education—and taxation policy discourage them from employment.

3. *Social democratic welfare regime* (i.e., Nordic countries such as Finland, Norway, and Sweden): These types of governments take the most responsibility for their citizens based on promoting the principles of equality and universalism. Sweden, for example, has a social democratic welfare regime where women are able to pursue full employment and receive the utmost support from the government. Bianchi et al. (1999), in describing these societies, state: "These countries have tax systems favoring women's employment, and a large public sector labor market in the areas of health, education, and welfare...[they] provide highly developed day care services and paid parental leave" (p. 6). A successful example of a social democratic state is Sweden. Swedish parents receive fifteen months of parental leave and have access to high quality, state run day care centers. The taxation system taxes the individual but not the family. All of these factors contribute to favorable incentives for women to stay employed.

Esping-Anderson's typology can be applied to many Western countries but its categorizations do not account for other types of government regimes. Olmsted (2005: 117) refers to King's work (2001), raising the question of whether Middle Eastern and Mediterranean countries constitute a fourth category, which she refers to as "familial" or "Mediterranean" model. This model describes many of the Mediterranean and Middle Eastern countries where families play the central role in providing many of the services that are often assigned to the state in other countries. Care for dependants, the ill, and the elderly is often provided by the family or extended family, independent of the state. Women often perform the role of primary care givers.

That women should assume these roles is encouraged and often-times enforced/demanded by cultural messages, governmental rules, and familial norms. Therefore employment outside of the home is highly discouraged for women.

IS PAID EMPLOYMENT EMPOWERING AND LIBERATING FOR WOMEN?

On one hand, it is argued that labor force participation is asso-ciated with women's empowerment because of the access it pro-vides to societal resources. Most of the feminist literature, as well as reports from the World Bank and the United Nations, portray women's attachment to the labor force as the main ingredient for their empowerment and higher status. Dubeck and Dunn (2002), in their study of women's work, list many reasons for examining women's employment. They argue that women's paid work is not only good for individual women (it is empowering and status enhancing) but also beneficial to the collective well-being of the society. Working women contribute to the production of goods and services but their participation in the workforce extends beyond advancing personal economics to the creation of jobs and new industries. For example, family and educational institutions are intensely affected by women's employment since employed women are not able to perform every familial task themselves. Therefore their services are often replaced by the development of new industries, such as child and elderly care institutions, extended school days for children, janitorial services, the growth of the fast food and restaurant industry, and so on.

It has also been argued that women's entry into the workforce strengthens their position in the political system, helping them understand their rights and boosting their political participa-tion both individually and collectively. Oftentimes grassroots organizations are formed by and for women to protect their interests in countries where they work in low-wage factory jobs. These countries include Hong Kong, Taiwan, India, Indonesia, Tunisia, and Morocco (Moghadam, 1999; Ross, 2008; Telhami et al., 2009). Studies of female garment workers in Bangladesh indicate that when women work side by side in factories, these locations become fertile grounds for sharing information and building social networks. For example, from these social networks, women learn about health-related issues and become more aware of contraceptive choices (Amin et al., 1998; Kabeer and Mahmud, 2004).

So, is paid unemployment empowering and liberating for women? The answer is that women's employment is not necessarily connected to their liberation and empowerment. In fact, employment is sometimes disempowering and exploitative of women. Olmsted (2005), in her analysis of paid work in the Arab nations, states:

> paid employment for women is no panacea, either for women themselves or for society in general. Even when they enter paid employment, women often remain more economically vulnerable than men, not only because they face discrimination and exploitative work conditions, but also because societies continue to assign them the generally unremunerated economic role of reproductive labor. (P. 112)

There is no doubt that women in many parts of the world are often exploited by their employers and oftentimes by their own family members, where they are used as unpaid and subjugated labor.

In the West, we see how women's employment has led to female empowerment and improved their social status, while in the MENA region female participation in the workforce has oftentimes left their social status unchanged. It is also worth pointing out that there are actually cases in which women's participation in the workforce is counterproductive. Women from lower socioeconomic status groups who end up in lower class jobs find their social status is further diminished. Sassen (1999) and Parrenas (2000, 2001) explain this as a phenomenon of the global labor market.[3]

IS AN INCREASE IN PAID WORKING WOMEN IN THE MENA REGION EVIDENCE OF EMPOWERMENT OR EXPLOITATION?

As was covered in chapter six, among the younger generation, the gap in educational attainment between women and men has narrowed tremendously in the MENA region. Furthermore, following the projections of modernization theory, many of the educated women are marrying later and having fewer children. In theory, higher education for women should lead to more employment opportunities. And yet, Bahramitash (2007), in her study of contemporary Iranian women and the changes in their social status over the past decades, points to a lack of connection between education and employment. Iranian society has not been able to provide jobs for many of these women. The unemployment rate was as high as 20 percent for females and 12 percent for males in 2000–2004. Algeria, as another example, reports its unemployment rate for both men and women increasing and staying unusually high (30 percent for both between 2000 and 2004) (see table 7.3 for unemployment statistics). It is all well and good to educate women, but if the underlying economy cannot support more workers an advanced education does not necessarily offer an advantage. Furthermore, in recent decades, the poverty rate among women has increased dramatically due to higher inflation, higher male and female unemployment rates, and higher incidences of women not marrying, marrying later, or getting divorced, which leaves them without a male to support them financially. Rising poverty rates and high inflation force many educated and less educated women to seek employment. But the question becomes at what level are they finding employment? Employed workers are often concentrated in particular sectors that contribute to gender segregation in the labor force. Female concentrated jobs are often lower status and lower paying jobs. In general, women are concentrated in public sectors in most of the MENA region. More than 50 percent of employed women in Jordan and Egypt and over 90 percent in Kuwait, for example, are public sector employees (Wahba, 2003).

If women, both educated and noneducated, are competing for low wages, low status jobs then Bahramitash (2007) argues that working "does not necessarily translate into economic empowerment for women" (p. 104). Simply because statistically more women are working does not mean they are seeing improvements in their wages or that overall they are a more economically empowered group. Rising employment for women in Iran and other countries in the region could

Table 7.3 Selected indicators of employment for men and women

| Country | Female labor force participation (% of total labor force) | | | Unemployment | | | |
| | | | | Total (% of total labor force) | | Female (% of female labor force) | |
	1980	1990	2000–2004	1990	2000–2004	1990	2000–2004
Algeria	20	23	30	19.8	29.8	15.9	29.7
Bahrain	11	17	19	—	—	—	—
Egypt	19	26	22	8.6	11	17.9	23.9
Iran	20	20	33	—	11.6	—	20.4
Iraq	16	17	19	—	28.1	—	16
Jordan	18	19	24	—	13.2	—	20.7
Kuwait	13	22	25	—	—	—	—
Lebanon	28	32	30	—	—	—	—
Libya	16	17	26	—	—	—	—
Morocco	21	24	25	15.8	10.8	—	—
Oman	15	11	16	—	—	—	—
Qatar	9	10	14	—	3.9	—	12.6
Saudi Arabia	8	11	15	—	5.2	—	11.5
Syria	23	26	30	—	11.7	—	24.1
Tunisia	19	21	27	15.3	14.3	—	—
Turkey	35	29	26	8.0	10.3	8.5	9.7
United Arab Emirates	5	10	13	—	2.3	—	2.6
Yemen	28	27	28	—	11.5	—	8.2
Region/ economic category							
MENA	20	—	27	—	13.6	—	—
Lower middle income	41	—	42	3.9	5.9	—	—
High income	39	—	44	5.6	5.5	5.5	5.4
United States	41	44	46	5.6	6.4	6.8	6.6

MENA: Middle East and North African region.

Source: The World Bank Group, GenderStats, Database of Gender Statistics, http://devdata. worldbank.org/genderstats/genderRpt.asp?rpt=profile&cty=BHR,Bahrain&hm=home. Retrieved on August 30, 2007.

be indicative of "economic exploitation rather than economic empowerment" (p. 104).

Table 7.3 shows patterns of women's employment and unemployment from 1980 to 1990 and 2000–2004. The first column lists eighteen individual members of the MENA region, and the second column lists female labor force participation as a percentage of the total labor force. In fifteen out of eighteen cases, female labor force participation has increased between 1980 and 2004. In Turkey we see a steady decline. In Egypt and Lebanon we see an initial increase between 1980 and 1990 followed by a decline by 2004. The same data, grouped by region, shows that overall in the MENA region female labor force participation has increased as is also witnessed in the United States. The lowest rate of female employment in the MENA region in 2000–2004 belongs to UAE (13 percent) and Saudi Arabia (15 percent). The highest rates are reported for Iran (33 percent), Algeria, Lebanon, and Syria (all 30 percent). Female labor force participation for the MENA region is as low as 27 percent. Despite the relative levels of rising employment for women, unemployment rates in the MENA region for both men and women are among the highest in the world indicating a high demand and a low supply of jobs. In Iran women's employment rate is 33 percent—the highest in the region (still low compared to countries in other regions) and the female unemployment rate is over 20 percent. In Syria the labor force participation of women is 30 percent, and the unemployment rate for women is 24 percent (a pattern similar to Iran). While the unemployment rate in high income countries is slightly lower for women than for men (6.8 percent for men and 6.6 for women in the United States), in the MENA region, women's employment rate is much lower than men's and their unemployment rate is much higher than men's. The highest recorded unemployment rates among these countries belong to Algeria, Egypt, Iran, Iraq, Jordan, and Syria. These countries also have a higher percentage of college educated women among their younger population (with the exception of Iraq), once again countering the modernization theory's positive correlation between higher education and higher labor force participation.

Income disparity between men and women in the MENA region is even more prevalent (table 7.2). For example, Kuwaiti men earn three times more than women, Omani men four times more, Saudi men five times more compared with a much smaller gap between men and women's earnings in the United States, Norway, and Sweden.

SOCIETAL NORMS, SOCIAL CONTRACTS, AND WOMEN'S WORK

Societies often have an implicit set of norms indicating how individuals should be cared for through the traditions of family and religion. For example, the patriarchal system gives men the ultimate control of the family members but also assigns them the responsibility of providing for their immediate and often extended families (elderly parents, sisters, nieces, and nephews in addition to their own nuclear family). Some interpretations of Sharia law state that men are economically responsible for women but women do not have the obligation to provide unpaid housework and have the right to be compensated for their work, and married women do not have an obligation to contribute to the household income. A study of women's paid employment and financial arrangements with their families in the United Arab Emirates shows that employed (mainly middle and upper middle class) married women were in control of their own money and did not have the obligation to share their income with their husbands. The expectation is that men are in charge of their family's finances but women are not obligated to work or share their income if they do work (Briegel and Zivkovic, 2008).

Societies also, to varying degrees, have explicit social contracts provided by the government. For example, governments set up tax systems in exchange for providing social services to their citizens. Members of a society might give up some things (certain rights, and monetary payments in the form of taxes) to their government in exchange for receiving social services. In societies with few or no explicit governmental social services, families and kinship systems perform these roles. For example, in Nordic countries with social democratic welfare regimes, the government takes responsibility for almost all social services including education, health, child, and elderly care. But in countries like those in the MENA region, with strong patriarchal family systems, societies rely on families and kinship systems to provide the care for children, the ill, and the elderly. It is often argued that it is financially beneficial for governments to justify and perpetuate patriarchal family norms, as is the tradition in many of the Middle East, South and East Asian societies.

In many of the countries in the MENA region, women's labor force participation drops when they enter marriage and the childbearing years since their primary role is considered to be caring for their family, per the strong patriarchal traditions of the region, and there is a lack of government-provided social services. Wahba (2003: 26) reports the following:

1. In Egypt, women's employment drops as soon as they enter marriage and their childbearing years (Assaad and El-Hamidi, 2002).
2. In Iran, married women have the lowest rate of participation compared to single and widowed women. Divorced women have the highest rate of participation in the labor force (Salehi-Isfahani, 2000a).
3. In Kuwait, single women between the ages of twenty-five and thirty-nine have twice the labor force participation as married women (30 versus 60 percent) (Shah and Al-Qudsi, 1990).

Another interesting twist to the MENA societies' women-work equation is that the relatively high male income levels made possible by the oil boom, directly or indirectly by means of remittances, "contributed to the preservation of the patriarchal family structure by making it [financially] unnecessary for women to seek paid employment outside the home" (Wahba 2003: 26).

In examining the labor force dynamics in the MENA region, we encounter unique situations. Overall, women in the MENA region are not fully included in the labor force. They experience a low rate of employment and high rate of unemployment as a group despite increasing education and reduced fertility rates. It should be mentioned that the process of modernization occurred gradually over three centuries in the Western world and allowed ample time for a gradual and unstoppable shift in social values and institutions. As modernization progressed, so did population sizes (changed from low population growth to high and then to almost no population growth—refer table 7.1). In the MENA region, modernization was spurred on by the global importance of oil and minerals. Its rapid expansion did not recreate the same environment that led to the development of the job market and industries as occurred in the Western modernization process. And so, with the population bulge that ensued, a greater conflict between traditional social values and institutions was experienced.

Today, in the MENA region, we see a hybrid modernization characterized by some modern industry giving rise to rapid national wealth and political importance struggling with firmly entrenched traditional social values and institutions aware of their potential extinction. We discussed neopatriarchy in chapter three and we need to revisit the discussion. Sharabi (1988) argues that patriarchy has become modernized in the MENA region to a new form which he refers to as neopatriarchy. Neopatriarchy argues that in the process of becoming modernized, some of the oil-producing Arab countries experienced a rapid economic development that did not follow the economic development path of Western nations. Therefore, only Western societies experienced modernization in a "pure" sense because it happened without interference from other nations. Furthermore, with respect to gender roles, neopatriarchy continues to define a woman's primary role as homemaker and mother. Therefore, changes in the level of industrialization have little effect on women's involvement in the market and do not change their social status.

Including women in the paid workforce will be advanced by a society if it is not facing economic and political failures and can support both men and women with jobs and social services. If the country is facing political turmoil and economic breakdowns, women's employment is not a priority. In those instances all sorts of cultural norms and ideological messages will be used to justify keeping women at home to attend to their families' care and well-being. Frequently however, women of lower socioeconomic status do not have the strong familial support and the societal system is also ill-equipped to protect them.

CHAPTER 8

LABOR MIGRATION, OIL REVENUE, AND
THEIR IMPACT ON WOMEN'S
EMPLOYMENT

The oil boom of the 1970s brought rapid success to the
Middle East. Prices of oil soared, leading to a sudden accumulation of wealth. The overflow of revenue had a dramatic
impact not only on the newly rich oil producing countries but
on the global economy as well.[1] One important consequence
was an influx of foreign labor to parts of the Middle East,
mainly from other Asian, Middle Eastern, and African nations
due to the abundance of well-paying jobs for all levels and skills.
By the mid-1990s, as much as 70 percent of the labor force
was foreign-born in the six Gulf Cooperation Council (GCC)
countries[2] (the countries with the highest share of foreign-born
workers were the UAE, Kuwait, and Qatar). The unusually
high proportion of foreign labor in the region represents the
integration of the oil exporting countries into the global economy since the 1960s. In the global economy, foreign workers
are a crucial part of the exchange of resources among nations.
A relatively recent pattern within developing countries is that
migrants are treated as exchangeable commodities between
nations and the migrant workers can be repatriated when no
longer needed (Sassen, 1988, 2007).

PRE- AND POST-1970S FLOW OF FOREIGN LABOR

Petroleum was initially discovered in Iran during the first decade of the twentieth century. By 1911, the British-Persian oil company (Anglo-Persian Oil Company—APOC) was producing oil in Iran. Oil was discovered next in Iraq after World War I, in Bahrain in 1932, and in Saudi Arabia in 1933. World War II intervened and delayed the discovery of petroleum in other parts of the region. Since the 1950s, most of the oil-producing nations have become less technologically and politically dependent on British and American oil companies and have accumulated wealth for the elite families and their governments (U.S. Library of Congress Country Studies, 2006) (see appendix A for the list of the top fifty oil-producing and oil-consuming countries in the world).

Prior to the 1970s, a relatively small pool of foreign labor existed in the Middle East.[3] Americans and Europeans held jobs in the oil export industry. Pakistanis, Sudanese, Egyptians, and Palestinians were often employed as doctors, nurses, and other professionals in small numbers. The foreign worker community was rather small but started to grow rapidly with the soaring oil prices in the early 1970s. In their description of the demographics of the labor migration in the GCC region, Martin and Widgren (1996) describe the flow of labor to the region:

> The post-1973 oil wealth encouraged the newly rich Middle Eastern governments to launch multi-billion dollar projects to build airports, roads, and housing, and to expand health care, education, and other service industries. Their native labor force was inadequate both in numbers and skills for implementing their government plans, and the countries turned to foreign sources of labor. The number of foreign workers in the six Persian Gulf states exploded, from 1.1 million in 1970 to 5.2 million in 1990. Another two million foreigners, primarily Egyptians, worked in Iraq. Foreigners became a majority of the labor forces and populations of many oil-exporting countries. (P. 34)

Today, a majority of the foreign workers in the Middle East are from South Asia and neighboring Arab countries. The largest single source of foreign workers in the MENA region is from Egypt. Egyptians work in different parts of the Middle East, especially in the GCC region. Other major labor exporting countries are Jordan, Yemen, and Sudan (Martin and Widgren, 1996; Shah, 1995). As table 8.1 indicates, the highest Net Migration Rate in the MENA region is among the GCC countries. Kuwait (15), Oman (16), Qatar (36) and UAE (35) show a substantial gain in their populations due to their pattern of in-migration. Algeria (-1), Iran (-3), Egypt (-2), Tunisia (-1), Yemen (-1) show a negative net migration rate—an indicator of population loss due to out-migration. Net migration rate for North America as a labor importing region is only 4. Comparing that rate to the migration rate in the GCC shows the magnitude of labor import/export in the MENA region.

Migrant workers in the GCC countries dominate three main sectors of the economy: construction, manufacturing, and utilities. The greatest decline has been in the construction sector since the peak of the construction boom in the 1970s and 1980s. In turn, the service sector has grown and absorbed a large percentage of immigrant workers (Birk et al., 1988). Today's GCC countries would be in a different state of development and industrialization if it were not for migrant workers. In particular the expansion of these countries' health and education sectors is mainly due to the inclusion of migrant workers (Shah, 1995). By the 1990s nearly 70 percent of the GCC labor force consisted of foreign workers, with UAE's foreign-born labor as high as 90 percent of their labor force (table 8.2). In countries such as Kuwait and UAE foreign workers constitute 84 percent and 90 percent of the labor force (table 8.2). Foreign-born labor constitutes 39 percent of the total population in the GCC (table 8.2) but 70 percent of the labor force (table 8.2). The extreme dependence of these countries on foreign labor is undeniable and would be very difficult to change. Shah (1995) explains the concerns regarding the high volume of migration and states that immigration is likely to continue in heavy volumes. Among the many reasons cited for the heavy flow of immigration are (i) the need to maintain the infrastructure, (ii) the reluctance of the native labor force to participate in productive and manual labor, (iii) the increased demand for domestic servants (p. 1001).

Table 8.1 Migration patterns in the MENA region, 2000–2001

Country	Net migration rate for MENA countries and other regions, 2001 (1)		Emigrants from the MENA region to OECD by level of education, 2000 (%) (2)		
	Net migration rate per 1,000 population, 2001	Projected population change, 2007–2050 (%)	Low-skilled (less than 8 years of schooling; %)	Medium-skilled (9–12 years of schooling; %)	High-skilled (13 years and more of schooling) %
Algeria	–1	47	77	9	14
Bahrain	7	56	—	—	—
Egypt	–2	61	18	23	59
Iran	–3	41	17	25	59
Iraq	–3	114	35	27	39
Jordan	7	71	16	28	56
Kuwait	15	87	12	20	68
Lebanon	–0	27	30	25	45
Libya	–0	57	23	23	54
Morocco	–2	43	71	17	13
Oman	16	42	22	15	63
Qatar	36	55	15	15	70
Saudi Arabia	0	80	13	22	65
Syria	2	75	31	25	44
Tunisia	–1	29	73	12	15
Turkey	0	20	—	—	—
United Arab Emirates	35	90	17	16	67
Yemen	–1	159	34	32	35
Region					
World	0	40	—	—	—
More developed	3	3	—	—	—
North America	4	38	—	—	—
Europe	2	–9	—	—	—
Less developed	–0	49	—	—	—
Less developed (excluding China)	1.8	61	—	—	—
Africa	2.4	107	—	—	—
Northern Africa	1.9	59	—	—	—
South America	1.5	38	—	—	—
Western Asia	2.0	65	—	—	—
South Central Asia	–0	56	—	—	—
United States	4	39	—	—	—

MENA: Middle East and North African region.

Note: Emigrants include all working age (25 years or older), foreign-born individuals living in an OECD country. Adding each row should total to 100 percent. The numbers were rounded.

Sources: *World Population Data Sheet*. 2007. Washington DC: Population Reference Bureau. Docquic and Marfouk (2005); Adams (2006).

Table 8.2 National and foreign population and labor force in GCC countries

	Bahrain	Kuwait	Oman	Qatar	Saudi Arabia	United Arab Emirates	GCC
Population of national- and foreign-born in GCC, 1997 (1)							
Nationals (* 1,000)	284	744	1,642	157	13,500	658	17,085
Foreign population (foreign workers + their dependents) (* 1,000)	236	1,409	614	365	6,000	2,038	10,662
Total (* 1,000)	620	2,153	2,256	522	19,500	2,696	27,747
% foreign population	39%	66%	28%	67%	31%	76%	39%
Percent of foreign work force relative to the total workforce (% for GCC means total of foreign and native) in the GCC countries, 1975–1997 (2)							
Foreign work force relative to the total workforce							
1975	46	70	54	83	32	84	47
1985	58	81	69	90	65	90	70
1995–97	62	84	62	82	64	90	70
Women as a percentage of the labor force, 1975–2000 (3)							
Women as percentage of the labor force	5	8	—	2	5	3	—
1975	11	13	5	7	8	5	—
1980	19	25	16	14	15	13	—
2000							

GCC: Gulf Cooperation Council countries.

Sources: (1) Willoughby (2005), table 2 and 7. (2) Shah (1995), table 1; World Bank Group, GenderStats database of gender statistics. 2006. Retrieved in August 12, 2006. http://devdata. worldbank.org/.

Female migrant workers, with a variety of skill levels, also constitute a relatively large percentage of the foreign workers holding jobs. Many are illiterate or barely literate and perform janitorial and domestic work (mainly women from Bangladesh, Pakistan, and Sri Lanka). Some are highly educated (mainly from other Arab countries such as Egypt) and hold jobs as teachers, nurses, and, sometimes, doctors serving the country's female population. In Kuwait, for example, the number of non-Kuwaiti women in the labor force increased from 13 percent in 1980 to 25 in 2000 within the last two decades. These workers primarily find employment as domestic servants and nurses (table 8.2). The highest percentage of non-Kuwaiti workers (men and women) are employed in maintenance-related occupations: that is, in infrastructure and personal services (Shah, 1995). In many of these countries, the native population is overqualified or is not willing to take low paid and low status jobs. Shah, in her description of the migrant and native population in Kuwait, states:

> As the educational level increases further among the Kuwaiti population, indigenous workers would be overqualified for occupations currently performed by illiterate foreign workers. Such jobs will be considered too lowly by nationals. Also in cultural terms, certain occupations (e.g., cleaning services) are now deemed to be purely non-Kuwaiti occupations, and participation in them would reduce the status of a Kuwaiti tremendously. (Pp. 1016–1017)

THE IMPACT OF LABOR MIGRATION ON RECEIVING AND SENDING COUNTRIES

There are conspicuous transformations in both sending and receiving countries when societies experience in- and out-migration. In the MENA region, emigration[4] has primarily been welcomed by governments of labor-exporting nations, for at least two reasons:

1. From the sending countries, the burden of providing jobs for a large number of the labor force is drastically reduced.
2. Remittances are sent home to the families of the workers. Countries such as Turkey, Egypt, and Jordan included the remittances as part of their national budget up until the 1990s. (This resulted in vulnerability to external economic events, and they were hit the hardest with the low demand for migrant workers and the decline in the flow of remittances).

Labor migration from labor-exporting countries (e.g., The Philippines, Morocco, Tunisia, Egypt, Sudan, Jordan, Lebanon, Syria, and Yemen) is considered a double-edged sword to the immigrants' country of origin. When their citizens return home, their governments are faced with an unexpected need to accommodate returning migrants. Since the wages are high in oil-producing countries, the returning migrants expect higher pay, comparable to what they were paid in the host countries (Hijab, 1988, 1994). In some instances, labor-exporting countries import labor to make up for their losses. For example, in Jordan, by the mid-1980s, some sixty thousand Egyptians were recruited as replacement migrants, working mostly in the agricultural sector. They replaced Jordanian workers who migrated to the Gulf countries for better-paying jobs (Hijab, 1988: 78). Hijab (1994) argues that if labor exporting countries do not supplement their own labor shortage with immigrant workers, the female employment of the native population might rise: (i) A rise in the cost of living, partly due to labor migration, might create a higher living standard due to remittances and therefore bring more women into the labor force. (ii) Women might also be encouraged to enter the labor force as a replacement for male migrants who have migrated to oil-producing nations for higher-paying jobs (e.g., the cases of Sudan, Jordan, and Iraq).

We should be reminded here that, as we discussed in previous chapters, MENA countries maintain a constant multifaceted effort to preserve the patriarchal system by limiting change in women's status. For example, The GCC countries' response to a significant loss of male laborers to more lucrative jobs across the borders was to bring in replacement male laborers from poorer or more overpopulated regional members. It is easy to hypothesize that this action by the GCC is an attempt to avoid the outcome that a similar change had on Western societies. During World War II, a significant proportion of the male population in the United States was relocated overseas for the war effort. This loss, and the rapid rise of the domestic military hardware industry, prompted the United States to move women away from their traditional role as homemakers and into the manufacturing workforce. This created a shift in women's status in the West, which within two decades sparked the women's liberation movement in the

1960s. If GCC countries did not replace their male citizens who migrated to high paying positions in oil-producing states with imported replacement labor, it might challenge the patriarchal system by encouraging women to enter the local labor force. One last effect of migration to high paying jobs outside the country is that the remittances sent home are in a higher valued currency, which helps create a higher standard of living for the families in the home country. Again, in previous chapters, and in the history of modernization theory, we see an increase in income (stronger economy) as being one avenue leading to changes in women's status including their entrance into the labor force.

Many of the immigrants, depending on their skill level, personal choice, and availability of opportunities, often end up in the oil-producing nations, while a large number also immigrate to North American and European countries. Immigrants from Lebanon make up the highest percentage of the total labor force in the MENA countries (15 percent), followed by Morocco (7.6 percent), Tunisia (5.4 percent), and Algeria (4.5 percent). Immigrants from the MENA region hold disparate levels of education and skills. A majority of immigrants from Algeria (76.7 percent), Tunisia (73 percent), and Morocco (76.6 percent) entering the Organization for Economic Cooperation and Development (OECD) countries are low-skilled laborers (table 8.1). In contrast, most of the immigrants entering OECD countries that came from Qatar (69.6 percent), UAE (67.3 percent), Kuwait (67.8 percent), Saudi Arabia (65 percent), Oman (63 percent), Egypt (59 percent), Iran (59 percent), Jordan (56 percent), and Libya (54 percent) are reported to be high-skilled workers, with thirteen or more years of schooling (table 8.1). This pattern reflects job opportunities for lower-skilled workers in oil-producing countries (absorbed by immigrant workers), but a shortage of job opportunities for more educated natives.

The question then is of why labor shortages in labor importing countries have not led to a greater integration of women into the labor force as is theoretically expected. According to Hijab (1988) three conditions are needed to promote women's gainful employment in a country: need, opportunity, and ability. An absence of any of the three could lead to a slower pace or lower integration of women into the labor force. In the face of those criteria the MENA region falls short on several fronts.

- Need: In oil-producing nations, sudden wealth meant a sharp rise in Gross National Product per capita. However, because of the high level of male income and the job security offered by the governments, women's financial contribution was probably not felt to be needed by families.
- Opportunity: Oil wealth also meant that the government could easily afford to hire foreign workers "despite the fact that this was felt to be a threat to the social fabric" (Hijab, 1988: 137). The reoccurring theme of patriarchal protectionism (as discussed in the previous chapters) is observed. Migrant workers entering the MENA oil-producing states have the potential to bring cultural changes. To avoid this migrants are subject to government controls that deny them the right to marry local women, bring their families, or start a family during their employment. Not only are they denied citizenship from the host country, but they can be deported when their employment ends or is terminated. The rapid change in the social structure and the perceived encroachment of foreign influences was probably the main factor reinforcing attachment to traditionalism's particularly rigid interpretation of gender roles (Hijab, 1994; Sharabi, 1988). Women's roles in that context were defined as mothers and wives, which tend to deflect the opportunity for women to be economically active.
- Ability: The sudden wealth created job opportunities in the modern sector. For decades (until recently), women in general were not prepared with proper education and skills to enter the modern labor force due to the disparity between male and female education and skill levels. The education gap in the past few decades has narrowed. However, as we saw in chapter six, despite women's great strides in educational achievement in the Middle East, they are kept out of the labor force due to reasons such as government's political and economic failures, high inflation and population explosion.

After accounting for the fact that the oil industry as a capital-intensive industry (due to its enormous wealth flow from oil) created many labor-intensive jobs in construction and oil industry suited for men (mainly taken by migrant workers), other reasons for the unchanging status of women vary from country to country in the MENA region. Governments in many of these countries insisted on preserving the patriarchal system, already in existence for centuries, in which women's status was solely defined by successfully maintaining the family's well-being. In other countries, a population explosion provided the labor force with more than enough men to fulfill the job market demands. If further labor was needed, it was imported from neighboring countries or South Asian countries with the legal stipulation that migrant workers could be denied citizenship and family rights, and sent home when no longer needed. And finally, some countries still experience political and/or economic failures in growing a diversified economy. While the oil industry brought in much needed revenue and created some jobs, failure to promote other industrial avenues made it difficult for the remaining unemployed men to find work.

An elaborate quantitative study of the MENA countries by Ross (2008) suggests that the underrepresentation of women in the workforce and politics is not because of Islam but is due to the effect of petroleum on the economies of these countries. In addition, Ross explains the unusually low status of women in oil-producing countries outside of the Middle East region (e.g., Azerbaijan, Botswana, Chile, Nigeria, and Russia) as also being connected to oil and mineral production. In his analysis of oil-rich and oil-poor countries, Ross (2008) emphasizes an economic condition called the Dutch Disease. The Dutch Disease describes the relationship between the decline in the manufacturing sector and exploitation of natural resources such as petroleum production and export of goods.[5] With the increase in wealth and revenues from natural resources (oil in this case), the traditional sector—also referred to as the traded sector (agriculture and manufacturing)—becomes less significant, while non-traded sectors (construction and services) becomes more significant in the economy (Corden and Neary, 1982).

To understand Ross's proposed theory that oil and mineral production alters the regional economy in a way that hurts women's status, we need to move beyond the popular stereotypical view of oil-producing nations as rich and therefore able to progress faster through modernization than non-oil-producing regions. While the term Dutch Disease was coined for the case of Holland, which saw a decline in manufacturing caused by the development of the Dutch oil industry, its application to the MENA region is more serious. Revenues from oil and mineral development cause an economic boom and drive up the currency exchange rate with foreign currencies. In the MENA region, a strong national currency makes it economically impossible to develop a diversified export manufacturing sector that, as we have seen in modernization of Europe and North America, is the sector that provides women entrance jobs into the workforce. For example, a product manufactured in Saudi Arabia, when exported to a foreign market, would be priced far above similar products made in less developed countries (e.g., China or India). Even within the oil-producing nation, locals will find imported goods cheaper than locally manufactured goods due to the difference in real currency rates.

To summarize Ross, and apply it to our thesis, we conclude that those MENA countries that suddenly went from poor and under-developed to wealthy never had a chance to progress through the full modernization process in which diversified industries were created as wealth accumulated and increased. We see more of a leap from agricultural and rural, to a brief single industrial development (oil and minerals) and then straight into a limited service oriented economy. To complicate matters more for women's status, those jobs suited to women (teaching, health care) were more appealing to imported foreign migrants due to the fact that local women would demand a higher wage than the one offered.

In applying Ross's Dutch Disease scenario to the MENA region, we see that without a long period of diversified industrialization, MENA women missed what has traditionally been the biggest single opportunity to improve their status. In Western societies, the massive scale and duration of industrialization created a real need for skilled workers and paved the way for women to join men in employment and to leave the rural/household life for the labor force thus gaining status and empowerment. The present reality in the MENA region is that the traded goods sector (agriculture and manufacturing) has either declined or failed to ever exist. The alternative, the non-traded sector (construction, service, and retail), is therefore the focus of major investments and will continue to employ men, whether fulltime nationals or temporary foreign workers. Also Ross, quoting Mammen and Paxton's work (2000), states that two main factors influence the number of women in the labor force. First, when wages are high women tend to lean toward paid work and therefore enter the workforce (considering that there are job opportunities). Second, the opposite effect can occur. When household income is high, women might be less willing to enter the labor force, since the household salary (most likely the husband's) is high.

Ross adds another dimension to the Dutch Disease: gender segregation in the labor force. He argues that women are given opportunities to enter the labor force but are only allowed to enter specific jobs in specific sectors, which permits employers to set different wages for men and women—lower wages for women and higher for men. In oil-rich countries, with the expansion of the oil economy, the non-traded sector (construction and services) will get a boost and support from the government and therefore expand where there is a concentration of male workers. Also oil-rich economies tend to expand their heavy industry; therefore, male jobs rather than female jobs expand and are protected (Ross, 2008).

The oil boom enabled a capital-intensive (versus labor-intensive) industrialization to develop and grow. Capital-intensive industry is that which requires large amounts of fixed assets and cash to operate. Capital-intensive industry is less beneficial to a native population's labor needs. Women's participation in the workforce is not encouraged and men are often given priority to occupy available jobs (Moghadam, 1993, 2004). The level of women's involvement in the paid labor force is best explained by each country's specific strategies that are adopted toward their economic development and their subsequent need for female labor.

The focus on women's issues (emphasis on traditionalism in the name of Islam) has often been a political strategy for these nations to deflect attention from their economic failures, high inflation rate, lack of ability to provide employment for everyone, and lack of adequate social services (Hijab, 1988; Moghadam, 1992b, 2004; Obermeyer, 1992). Religious ideology, cultural beliefs, and traditional principles cannot be argued to be the one and only reason for women's labor force lagging behind in these countries. Countries such as Saudi Arabia, as one of the top oil producers of the world, did not require female labor in order to grow and develop economically (in a form of capital-intensive industry). By contrast, countries such as Indonesia (oil-poor, majority Muslim) and Tunisia (no oil, majority Muslim) have developed their economy through labor-intensive industrial production, took advantage of their female labor and therefore are characterized by a higher rate of female labor force participation and women's political participation (Ross, 2008). In the oil-rich countries, the government controls the hiring of the foreign labor, which has become a permanent practice in those countries and a crucial part of the fabric of their industrialization and modernization. As Gross National Product continued to rise and to supply a relatively high level of income for men, it reinforced the attachment of these societies to traditionalism, conservatism, and Islamic fundamentalist ideology (Moghadam, 2004). Experiencing rapid population growth (as high as 3–4 percent) and high male and female unemployment, these societies willingly and openly adopted Islamization of the state and embraced traditional gender roles.

APPENDIX A: OIL PRODUCTION AND CONSUMPTION BY COUNTRY, 2003

Oil production by country			Oil consumption by country		
Rank	Countries	Oil production by country (Bbl/day)	Rank	Countries	Oil consumption by country (Bbl/day)
1	Saudi Arabia	9,475,000	1	United States	20,730,000
2	Russia	9,400,000	2	China	6,534,000
3	United States	7,610,000	3	Japan	5,578,000
4	Iran	3,979,000	4	Germany	2,650,000
5	China	3,631,000	5	Russia	2,500,000
6	Mexico	3,420,000	6	India	2,450,000
7	Norway	3,220,000	7	Canada	2,294,000
8	Canada	3,135,000	8	Korea, South	2,149,000
9	Venezuela	3,081,000	9	Brazil	2,100,000
10	United Arab Emirates	2,540,000	10	France	1,970,000
11	Nigeria	2,451,000	11	Mexico	1,970,000
12	Kuwait	2,418,000	12	Italy	1,881,000
13	Iraq	2,130,000	13	Saudi Arabia	1,845,000
14	United Kingdom	2,075,000	14	United Kingdom	1,827,000

Continued

Oil production by country			Oil consumption by country		
Rank	Countries	Oil production by country (Bbl/day)	Rank	Countries	Oil consumption by country (Bbl/day)
15	Libya	1,720,000	15	Spain	1,573,000
16	Angola	1,600,000	16	Iran	1,510,000
17	Brazil	1,590,000	17	Indonesia	1,168,000
18	Algeria	1,373,000	18	Taiwan	965,000
19	Kazakhstan	1,300,000	19	Netherlands	946,700
20	Indonesia	1,136,000	20	Thailand	900,000
21	Qatar	790,500	21	Australia	877,300
22	India	785,000	22	Singapore	800,000
23	Malaysia	770,000	23	Turkey	715,100
24	Argentina	745,000	24	Belgium	641,000
25	Oman	740,000	25	Egypt	590,000
26	Egypt	700,000	26	Venezuela	560,000
27	Australia	530,000	27	Malaysia	515,000
28	Colombia	512,000	28	South Africa	502,000
29	Ecuador	493,200	29	Argentina	470,000
30	Azerbaijan	477,000	30	Poland	445,700
31	Equatorial Guinea	420,000	31	Greece	435,700
32	Syria	405,000	32	United Arab Emirates	400,000
33	Vietnam	400,000	33	Iraq	377,000
34	Yemen	387,500	34	Sweden	362,400
35	Sudan	344,700	35	Philippines	342,000
36	Denmark	342,000	36	Kuwait	335,000
37	Gabon	268,900	37	Portugal	332,000
38	Congo	267,100	38	Pakistan	324,000
39	Thailand	230,000	39	Nigeria	290,000
40	South Africa	229,900	40	Hong Kong	285,000
41	Chad	225,000	41	Ukraine	284,600
42	Brunei	219,300	42	Austria	282,000
43	Turkmenistan	213,700	43	Colombia	269,000
44	Bahrain	188,300	44	Switzerland	268,100
45	Germany	167,400	45	Israel	249,500
46	Trinidad & Tobago	150,000	46	Norway	244,300
47	Italy	145,100	47	Chile	238,000
48	Uzbekistan	142,000	48	Libya	237,000
49	Japan	125,000	49	Puerto Rico	234,000
50	Peru	120,000	50	Algeria	233,000

Note: Highlighted countries are Muslim majority countries (50% or more Muslim).
Source: http://www.nationmaster.com/graph/ene_oil_pro-energy-oil-production, retrieved on June 10, 2006.

PART III

CONCLUSION, DISCUSSION, AND CASE STUDIES

CHAPTER 9

CONCLUSION

INTRODUCTION

Muslim societies reflect a complex set of cultural, political, and demographic patterns, and understanding the process of change within Muslim societies requires an in-depth analysis of the changes within their social context. Rather than accept the common myth that women's lack of social status in the MENA region is solely a consequence of Islam, the previous chapters questioned and examined women's status as a consequence of societal and demographic changes such as the increased educational attainment of men and women, declining fertility rates, in- and outflows of migration to and from oil-producing countries, the consistently lower status of women, and women's low employment participation. Furthermore, women's roles in MENA societies, women's status, and women's rights—or lack of them, are entangled in a complicated patchwork of social customs, Sharia, and civil laws influenced by Western European legal precedents. And then there is the influence of the relatively recent influx of oil wealth and the complex ways in which patriarchal systems are intertwined and often embedded in predominantly male dominated Islamic governments, and the emergence of the MENA region's influence in global politics and the global economy. While it cannot be denied that Islam is a powerful cultural, religious, and political force it certainly is not the sole factor contributing to the subjugation of women's rights in the Middle East.

THEORETICAL BACKGROUND

After examining the demographic changes in the MENA region that modernization theories of economic development offer as triggers for change, it became clear that, generally, in MENA societies the consequences have not been in agreement with the theory. In many of the MENA countries, high fertility rate have dropped, educational attainment of women has increased (at an astounding rate among the younger generation for both men and women), and mortality rates have declined but over-all women's status has not improved as much as expected and still lags. There are few job opportunities available for women in the formal labor force, and women have a persistently low level of political participation. Although access to resources is an important aspect of women's access to power and higher status in Western societies, it is not the only criteria for equality. A study of Lebanese and Iranian women, mentioned in chapters four and five, indicated that despite their improved educational attainment, women's social status has not improved (Lattouf, 2004; Shavarini, 2006).

All the facts and data presented in this book should allow us to debunk some common beliefs regarding women's status in the MENA region. First, 'Modernization' (as defined in the typical studies of European and North American societies) is not a natural process that all societies go through as they transition from agricultural to industrial and eventually to postindustrial economies. Second, process of modernization, born from studies based on European and North American history, applies only to those areas specifically and deviates in other regions of the world including the MENA region. The Western world went through modernization and experienced a set of results that is particular to the social, cultural, and economic realities unique to them. What sets the MENA region apart from the West is what follows:

1. In most of the MENA countries there is no formal, deliberate separation of church and state. The results are laws controlling all aspects of life that are based on historical ideologies; not a dynamic ideology that is constantly adjusted to better serve the changing realities affecting the population.

2. The industrialization and modernization processes in the MENA were either inadequate due to lack of resources, which in the West fueled the social changes for women, or too fast to allow the culture and people to acclimatize thus yielding little or no change in women's social status. Some MENA countries, with high fertility rates, few natural resources, very limited oil industry to develop, were unable to build up a diversified export manufacturing industry to employ what became large populations (i.e., Yemen—see more on Yemen later in this chapter). With societal stability at risk, patriarchy, Islam and cultural tradition became intertwined to control women's status for the benefit and protection of the state (i.e., the male elite). Other MENA countries went through such a rapid increase in wealth due to the discovery of oil and the global reliance on energy that those societies never completed a long and comprehensive modernization process. As I pointed out, these suddenly wealthy nations went through a brief single industrial phase (oil) and then changed right into a service economy ruled by capital-intensive investments. The speed and intensity of this process deprived women of the time and cultural forces necessary to inspire and cement an improvement in their social status. The explanation by Ross (2008) (Dutch Disease explained in chapter eight) shows how these oil exporting nations will never have the chance to create the vast variety of export-manufacturing industries that would have required, as seen in Western modernization, the integration of women into the labor force and the eventual improvement in their social status. The hypothesis, at this point, is that had the MENA proceeded through a Western-type modernization (without Western interference in their politics and economy), the economic forces of growth would have created a new ideology of government.

3. Western modernization was not reproduced, in toto, in the MENA region. The reason is not because of Islam as much as it was the timing. Europe and North America were the first areas to progress from agricultural to industrial societies. Those regions that followed afterward, the MENA, for example, had their industrialization processes (i.e., modernization)

altered by the forces I outlined in the sections on dependency theory and world systems theory. Rather than develop their own resources, manufacture products for export, and accumulate all the resulting wealth for domestic reinvestment, MENA oil producers modernized their economies through dependent relationships with the more technologically developed oil-consuming nations (which benefitted the Western world). A significant portion of the profits produced through MENA resource development was removed from the economy and exported to Western developed nations with no gain for the local MENA populations.

4. If we differentiate the previously defined dependency theory as the "Primary Dependency Theory" (i.e., transcontinental dependency) we can now introduce what we could refer to as the "Secondary Dependency Theory" (i.e., interregional dependency). In the primary dependency we see transnational companies from the first developed region (Europe and North America) exploiting the natural resources of the second region to develop (MENA oil nations). Significant value from the dependent countries is transferred to the economies of the developed countries. While examining the interrelationships between MENA countries (oil-producing, labor-deficient versus non-oil-producing), it became apparent that a similar system of dependency (exploitation of the less developed) had been created within the MENA. As countries such as Saudi Arabia, Kuwait, and United Arab Emirates, for example, became suddenly very wealthy (through dependency on Western oil-consuming economies), they fueled their growth and wealth accumulation by exploiting the abundance of inexpensive and available labor from other MENA, South and East Asian countries that lacked oil deposits and who represent the tertiary level of dependency. The national economies of countries such as Turkey, Egypt, and Jordan grew economically partially due to the remittances being sent home by workers migrating to the oil-producing nations. The result was an increase in the standard of living, and the need for these labor exporting nations to, in turn, import even cheaper labor from poorer areas to replace workers who had emigrated. Although these

labor exporting nations benefit from the wealth of the developing oil-producing nations, labor exportation does not build long-term stability as the labor pools are subject to changes in the global economy. The dependency theorists would see this situation as capitalist control of the less developed countries. A reflection of all three levels of dependency between countries is useful to illustrate the stratification, on a social status level, that has afflicted women in these same areas. Primary dependency level is evident in MENA oil-producing countries depending on Western oil-consuming countries (i.e., less developed nations depending on more developed ones). Secondary dependency level is evident in MENA labor exporting countries depending on MENA oil-producing countries. A tertiary dependency level exists between the less developed MENA countries depending on MENA labor exporting countries. Table 9.1 illustrates these three levels:

The following sections present a summary of each of the socio-demographic characteristics in the MENA countries (presented in detail in chapters two–eight). Afterward I will apply these conclusive summaries specifically to six individual MENA countries (Iran, Libya, Saudi Arabia, Tunisia, United Arab Emirates, and Yemen) that differ from one another in geographic location, economic base, demographic and modernization characteristics, and cultural history.

Fertility

The MENA region has succeeded in lowering its fertility rate and improving both men's and women's educational attainment. For women, reduced fertility is often associated with

Table 9.1 Different levels of dependency within the MENA region

Dependency level	Developed country	Less-developed country
Primary	Western oil consumers	MENA oil producers
Secondary	MENA oil producers	MENA labor exporters
Tertiary	MENA labor exporters	MENA less developed

MENA: Middle East and North African region.

higher status and increased access to resources. Access to family planning programs and health care facilities helps reduce fertility, leads to rising employment participation, and can increase women's autonomy and social status. Although the region is experiencing one of the highest population growth rates in the world, most countries in the MENA region have reduced their fertility rates (and mortality) drastically. However, the aftermath of those previously higher rates of fertility is that many of the MENA countries still have a disproportionately young population to educate, employ, and to provide with social services for decades to come.

In many of these societies, reproductive behavior is a function of the sociopolitical context rather than the impact of the Islamic influence. Although Islam does not prohibit the practice of family planning and does not encourage high fertility, the pro-natalist orientation of Islam is based not on direct injunctions, but indirectly through the political conditions created which are conducive to high fertility (Fagley, 1965; Obermeyer, 1992). By removing economic, social, and cultural barriers, governments play an important role in facilitating the use of health and family planning services, which in turn have been reducing fertility and mortality rates. Countries such as Algeria and Iran saw fertility decline dramatically while experiencing the rise and domination of Islamic fundamentalism (Fargues, 2003). I used the example of Yemen and Iran, which had experimented with different strategies over the course of several decades to increase or decrease their fertility rate. For example, in the case of Yemen, a large percentage of Yemeni women believe that Islam does not condone the use of contraception and are reluctant to seek birth control methods as it is considered "un-Islamic." Also the Yemeni government has made no effort to control and prevent the country's high fertility rate, high child mortality rate, and high maternal mortality; in fact, they deploy ideologies in the name of Islam to reinforce the rule of high fertility. Yemen's TFR is 7.2, the highest in the MENA region and one of the highest in the World (table 9.2). On the opposite end of the spectrum, the governments of Egypt and Iran have played a crucial role in implementing successful family planning programs. In Iran, for example, religious leaders

Table 9.2 Comparative analysis of six select MENA countries by socio-demographic and political characteristics

Select MENA countries	Iran	Libya	Saudi Arabia	Tunisia	United Arab Emirates	Yemen
Demographic characteristics (1)						
Muslim (Sunni, Shiite; %)	98 (Sunni 10, Shiite 88)	98 (Sunni 96)	100 (Sunni 90, Shiite 10)	98 (Sunni 99.7)	96 (Sunni 81, Shiite 15)	99%(Sunni 70, Shiite 30)
Population mid-2007 (millions)	71.2	6.27	27.6	10.2	4.4	22.4
Female population (% of total), 2003	49.8	48.4	46.0	49.5	35.0	49.0
Rate of natural increase, 2007	1.2	2.0	2.7	1.1	1.5	3.2
Projected population change (%), 2007–2050	41	57	80	29	90	159
Percent urban, 2006	85	85	81	65	74	26
Energy use per capita (kg oil equivalent), 2002	2,044	3,433	5,775	846	9,609	221
GNI PPP per capita (US $), 2002	—	—	16,620	8,490	23,990	920
Political leadership indicators (2)						
Women as % of parliament,						
1995	4	—	—	7	0	1
2004	3	—	0	23	0	0
Women as % of ministerial & sub-ministerial officials, 1998	1	1	0	8	0	0
GDI rank, 2003	106	61	73	91	48	148
Select fertility and health-related indicators (3)						
Life expectancy at birth						
Male	71	71	73	72	77	59
Female	76	76	77	76	81	62
Total fertility rate	2.0	3.9	5.7	2.1	3.5	7.2

Continued

Table 9.2 Continued

Select MENA countries	Iran	Libya	Saudi Arabia	Tunisia	United Arab Emirates	Yemen
Percent births attended by skilled personnel	90	94	91	91	99	22
Percent births conducted in health facilities	88	94	91	90	99	16
Maternal death per 100,000 live births	37	75	23	70	3	350
Abortion policy	Prohibited	Prohibited	Some restrictions	Liberal	Prohibited	Prohibited
Percent women married and percent women using cContraception, by different age groups (4)						
Percent women married, 15–19 years old	16	1	7	1	8	26
Percent women married, 20–24 years old	—	12	39	14	40	70
Percent married women, 15–49, using any method of contraception	74	45	32	63	28	21
Percent married women, 15–49, using modern contraception	56	26	29	53	24	10
Literacy indicators (5, 6)						
Percent illiterate (15 years or older), 2000						
Female	31	32	33	39	21	75
Male	17	9	17	19	25	33
Percent illiterate (15–24 years old), 2000–2004						
Female	9	7	10	11	6	6
Male	4	0.05	5	3	13	13

Continued

Table 9.2 Continued

Select MENA countries	Iran	Libya	Saudi Arabia	Tunisia	United Arab Emirates	Yemen
Literate women as percentage of literate men (15–24, 2000–2004)	95	94	96	93	108	60
Percent enrolled in primary school, 2000						
Female	85	117	—	115	99	61
Male	88	115	—	120	99	96
Percent enrolled in secondary school Female,						
1985	36	57	31	32	55	—
1993–1997	73	—	57	63	82	14
2000–2003	75	108	65	81	82	27
Male,						
1985	54	61	48	46	55	—
1993–1997	81	—	65	66	77	53
2000–2003	79	102	73	78	77	65
Women as share of university enrollment (%), 2000	47	48	56	48	—	21
Work and income indicators, 2000–2004 (7)						
Women's paid work:						
Non-agri. sector	—	—	14.0	—	12.7 0.1	5.8
Agri. sector	—	—	1.8	—		—
Female labor force participation (% of total labor force)	33	26	15	13	27	28
Estimated earned income (PPP US$)						
Female	2,599	—	4,222	3,377	6,041	365
Male	9,301	—	21,141	9,359	28,223	1,201
Income disparity between men and women (%)	28	—	20	36	21	30

Continued

Table 9.2   Continued

Select MENA countries	Iran	Libya	Saudi Arabia	Tunisia	United Arab Emirates	Yemen
Migration and oil production data (8)						
Oil producer ranking in the world (out of 50), 2003	#4	#15	#1	—	#10	#34
Percent of foreign workers among total work force, 1995–1997	NA	NA	64	NA	90	NA
Percent foreign population, 2001	NA	NA	31	NA	76	NA
Net migration rate per 1,000 population, 2001	-3	-0	0	-1	35	-1
Projected population change, 2007–2050	41	57	80	90	29	159

MENA: Middle East and North African region.

Source: Willoughby, 2005. "A Quiet Revolution in the Making? The Replacement of Expatriate Labor through the Feminization of the Labor Force in GCC Countries," table 2.

played a crucial role in sending out messages of *fatwas* (religious rulings) in favor of modern contraception. Government health care facilities distribute contraceptive devices and therefore make them available to couples from all levels of economic and social classes. The government has gone even further with their progressive approach in that the sole focus is not on women's responsibility for reducing fertility, they also place a great deal of importance on the men's roles in reducing fertility (Iran's TFR is 2.0 and one of the lowest in the world).

In general, most MENA countries provide direct access to family planning services (UN Report, World Population Policies, 2003) and most have succeeded in lowering their fertility rates for the past two decades. Abortion policies in the region vary from one country to another (see table 5.2 in chapter five). While most MENA countries prohibit abortion, countries such as Tunisia and Turkey have implemented liberal policies and the rest fall in the middle by placing some restrictions on abortion but not completely banning its practice. Abortion is strictly restricted (prohibited unless to save a woman's life) in Egypt, Iran, Iraq, Lebanon, Libya, Oman, Syria, United Arab Emirates, and Yemen.

Education

Modernization theory shows a strong relationship between increased access to education and positive changes in women's status. In the MENA region, sometimes the outcome of women's improved access to education deviates from the expectations of the modernization perspective, while other times we will see that the effects of women's education are rendered ineffective due to the dominant influence of cultural forces.

Roughly half of the countries in the MENA region have succeeded in significantly reducing illiteracy among their younger generations of women and men (nine of the eighteen countries within the MENA region report illiteracy rates of less than 10 percent for both boys and girls aged fifteen–twenty-four years). Those countries are Bahrain (1 percent), Iran (9 percent), Jordan (1 percent), Kuwait (7 percent), Lebanon (7 percent), Libya (7 percent), Oman (4 percent), Qatar (3 percent), and Turkey (6 percent). Iraq (71 percent), Yemen (54 percent), Morocco (42 percent), and Egypt (37 percent) still have a significant population of women in the fifteen–twenty-four age bracket who are illiterate (table 6.1 in chapter six). The illiteracy rate among women over fifteen is still high in several other countries in the MENA where women are roughly twice as likely as men to be illiterate in that age group (UNIFEM, 2004; Olmsted, 2005). Thus, the gender gap in providing education is closing in the MENA region. Most children in the region are enrolled in primary school (91 percent of girls and 100 percent of boys), but not all countries have been able to provide equal access to secondary school enrollment. Only 62 percent of girls and 71 percent of boys were enrolled in secondary school (table 9.2). Countries such as Libya and Bahrain have an impressive close to 100 percent rate for secondary school enrollment while Syria, Morocco, and Yemen show rates of 42, 36, and 27 percent for female enrollment in secondary school, respectively. However, in the two decades between 1980 and early-to-mid-2000, many countries experienced a dramatic jump in the enrollment of both male and female students in secondary school. For example, in 1985, 57 percent of women in Libya were enrolled in secondary school compared with 108 percent in year 2000. Oman and Tunisia provide other great examples; only 18 percent of girls in Oman and 32 percent in Tunisia were enrolled in secondary school in 1985. By the year 2000, 78 and 81 percent of girls were enrolled in Oman and Tunisia, respectively. Women's share of university enrollment is impressive in some of the GCC countries (Saudi Arabia, 56 percent; Oman, 58 percent; Bahrain, 60 percent; Kuwait, 68 percent; and Qatar, 73 percent) and low for Yemen and Iraq (20 and 34 percent, respectively) (table 6.2, chapter six).

A society's investment in education is generally assumed to pay off in the creation of more jobs (mainly in the nonagricultural sector) and better educated individuals in the workforce. For a society to receive returns on its investments on education, it needs to build a skilled and flexible labor force. Contrary to expectations, the MENA region's substantial investment in education has not been paying off as expected. There is little evidence that education has contributed to economic growth in the region (Nabli, 2002). The high rate of women's access to secondary and higher education in most of the MENA region is impressive although much improvement is still needed. According to modernization theorists and based on the experience of many Western societies, more educated women are more empowered women. They claim that as educational access for women improves, it creates more favorable conditions for women to enter the labor force. Therefore the number of women working increases with a higher degree of industrialization (Durand, 1975). Social and cultural changes such as marriage at a later age, declining fertility rates, and a demand for a more educated labor force, all contribute to a larger supply of female workers. The demand for a more educated labor force in modernizing societies is generally assumed to work in women's favor since modernization also increases women's access to better jobs.

And yet, as women's education level has increased in the MENA region, their labor force participation has not increased as expected. As of year 2000, women's formal employment in the MENA region was as low as 27 percent, which is accompanied by a staggering unemployment rate—sometimes as high as 30 percent. Within the region, the GCC countries show the lowest rate of women's employment (table 7.3 in chapter seven). In turn, as women in the region have become more educated, their labor force participation has not increased as expected. The low rate of women's employment (despite their improved educational attainment and lower fertility) results from their lack of improved social status (Lattouf, 2004; Shavarini, 2006). Despite women's high level of education, due to economic stagnation and regional political problems, the governments enforce traditional roles and values on women and run campaigns to legitimize discrimination against them. There is no doubt that the fact that these women have access to higher education contributes to the improvement of their status. On the other hand, if their status is not improved on a societal level, their higher education credentials will not help them to get far in the job market. Lattouf's observation (2004) of why families support their daughters' higher educational attainment despite the questionable rate of economic return is about the relations of women to men; families support their daughter's higher education as a way to improve their daughter's chances of finding a suitable husband of a similar or higher social status, which in turn adds to the families' collective social status.

Employment

A vast body of feminist literature indicates that women's paid work is not only empowering and "status enhancing" but beneficial to the collective well-being and it is an important aspect of the production of goods and services in societies. Women's entry into the workforce is also argued to strengthen their position in the political system, helps them understand their rights, and boosts their political and collective action. However, another body of literature indicates that women's employment can also be disempowering and exploitative of women. Their labor is often exploited by their employers and oftentimes by their own family members, where they are used as unpaid and subjugated labor. From the global point of view, different tiers of women are exploited in the global economy even more so.

Therefore, as much as women's labor force participation has been assumed to contribute to their liberation and empowerment, in the MENA region, it is not obvious that employment is beneficial to women and their social status. If the society has not set up "social contracts" outside of the family and the kinship system, employment is not as attractive for women. There is little incentive for women to work outside of their homes if they are still held accountable for all the domestic responsibilities that traditionally have fallen to them (see chapter seven). Societies arrange "social contracts" as guidelines to clarify an individual's and a society's responsibilities. They are set up as an exchange of goods and services. For example, in the Nordic countries the government takes responsibility for almost all social services including education, health care, child care, and elder care. In societies with few or none of these services, as is the case in most Muslim countries, families and kinship systems meet these needs. In fact, in societies dominated by patriarchal family systems, women are expected to fulfill most of the familial responsibilities. Whereas in nonfamilial regimes, that is to say, countries with social-democratic governments, the government would be expected to provide at least some of those services. Therefore, it is beneficial for governments to justify and perpetuate patriarchal family norms as is done in many of the MENA societies. In terms of women's position in the region, a "patriarchal gender contract" (Moghadam, 2004; Wahba, 2003) or "sexual contract" (Pateman, 1988; Olmsted, 2005) is argued to be the main factor determining participation or inhibition of women's involvement in the modern labor force (chapters two, three, and five). Women's status in society is the key determinant of their access to societal resources, which appears to be low in the MENA region.

Societies might have set up certain arrangements through the patriarchal system to care for women and children but once modernization is in place, compounded by economic and political failures, women have no guarantees of social and cultural support in these societies.

On the other hand, the unemployment rate in the region for both men and women is among the highest in the world, indicating a high demand for and a low supply of jobs. In the region, women's employment rate is much lower than men's while their unemployment rate is much higher than men's indicating the multiple reasons for their lack of participation in the workforce. The unemployment rates for women are highest in Algeria, Egypt, Iran, Iraq, Jordan, and Syria. These countries also have a higher percentage of college educated women amongst their younger population. The income disparity between men and women in the region is even more dramatic; the gap is much wider than in other regions. For example, Kuwaiti men earn three times more than women, Omani men four times more than women, Saudi men five times more than women (table 9.2).

In sum, women enter the paid workforce when the country is politically stable and has a diversified and prosperous economy enabling it to provide jobs and salaries to both men and women. When, instead, there is political instability or a lack of economic growth (or an economy based on a sole industry—oil) women's employment and improvements of their social status loses momentum and is actually discouraged. Cultural norms and ideological messages will be used to maintain the status quo; a woman's duty is to her family. In many cases, in exchange for their services and care giving, women are taken care of through the patriarchal kinship system (see chapter four for more on women's status). Women with lower socioeconomic status, however, might not have strong kinship support and cannot rely on their male family members in case of economic need. They are among the most disadvantaged groups in the region.

Oil

Although oil per se is not one of the markers that modernization theory identifies, the emergence of oil wealth in the region cannot be discounted. For many countries the discovery of oil led to a transformation of their role in the global economy. Soaring oil prices made it possible for the governments to enjoy enormous flows of revenue and labor to their countries—affecting their local economies while influencing the global economy (see chapter eight). Many of the migrant workers come from other Asian, Middle Eastern, and African nations due to the abundance of relatively well-paying jobs for all levels and skills.

After accounting for the fact that the oil industry as a capital-intensive industry (due to its enormous wealth flow from oil) created many labor-intensive jobs in construction suited for men (mainly taken by migrant workers), other reasons for the unchanging status of women vary from country to country in the MENA region. Governments in many of these countries insisted on preserving the patriarchal system, already in existence for centuries, in which women's status was solely defined by successfully maintaining the family's well-being. In other countries, a population explosion provided the labor force with more than enough men to fulfill the job market demands. If further labor was needed, it was imported from neighboring countries or South Asian countries with the legal stipulation that migrant workers could be denied citizenship and family rights, and sent home when no longer needed. And finally, some countries still experience political and/or economic failures in growing a diversified economy. While the oil industry brought in much needed revenue and created some jobs, failure to promote other industrial avenues made it difficult for the remaining unemployed men to find work. Thus, the underrepresentation of women in the workforce and politics is not because of Islam but it could be argued that it is due to the effect of petroleum on the economies of these countries (Ross, 2008). In addition, Ross explains the unusually low status of women in oil-producing countries outside of the Middle East region (e.g., Azerbaijan, Botswana, Chile, Nigeria, and Russia) as also being connected to oil and mineral production. In his analysis of oil-rich and oil-poor countries, Ross (2008) emphasizes an economic condition called the Dutch Disease. The Dutch Disease describes the relationship between the decline in the manufacturing sector and exploitation of natural resources such as petroleum production and export of goods. With the increase in wealth and revenues from natural resources (oil in this case), the traditional sector—also referred to as the traded sector (agriculture and manufacturing)—becomes less significant, while non-traded sectors (construction and services) becomes more significant in the economy (Corden and Neary, 1982).

The oil boom enabled a capital-intensive (versus labor-intensive) industrialization to develop and grow. A capital-intensive industry requires large amounts of fixed assets and cash to operate. Also, capital-intensive industry is less beneficial to a native population's labor needs. Women's participation in the workforce is not encouraged and men are often given priority to occupy available jobs (Moghadam, 1993, 2004). The level of women's involvement in the paid labor force is best explained by each country's specific strategies for their economic development and their subsequent need for female labor.

The emphasis on traditionalism in the name of Islam has often been a political strategy for these nations to deflect attention from their failed economic strategies, the consequences of population explosion, and the government's limited ability to provide employment and adequate social services (Hijab, 1988; Moghadam, 1992b, 2004; Obermeyer, 1992). Religious ideology, cultural beliefs, and traditional principles cannot be argued to be the one and only reason for women's labor force and social status lagging behind in these countries. Countries such as Saudi Arabia, as one of the top oil producers of the world, did not require female labor in order to grow and develop economically (in a form of capital-intensive industry). In contrast, countries such as Indonesia (oil-poor, majority Muslim) and Tunisia (no oil, majority Muslim) developed their economy through labor-intensive industrial production and took advantage of their female labor. These countries are characterized by a higher rate of female labor force participation and women's political participation (Ross, 2008). In the oil-rich countries, the government controls the hiring of foreign labor, which has become a permanent practice in those countries and a crucial part of the fabric of their industrialization and modernization.

Experiencing rapid population growth (as high as 3–4 percent growth rate) and high male and female unemployment, some of the MENA countries (e.g., Saudi Arabia) adopted Islamization of the state to preserve traditional gender roles.

CASE STUDIES OF SIX DIVERSE COUNTRIES IN THE MENA REGION: IRAN, LIBYA, TUNISIA, SAUDI ARABIA, UNITED ARAB EMIRATES, AND YEMEN

A common *misconception*, debunked throughout the book, is that women's social status in the MENA region is the direct result of the presence of Islam. If this assumption were true, women's status across the MENA region would be found to be relatively homogeneous with regards to female demographics such as fertility and mortality, educational attainment, participation in the labor force, earning potential, political participation, and social status in general. While Islam is present in each of these societies, it affects women's status to different degrees and it is not the driving force behind societal development. At the start of modernization, Islam and traditions of patriarchal rule became intertwined with the more powerful political and economic realities. Economic development and political control, aided by the preexisting patterns offered by Islam, are actually the stronger forces at work in defining women's status in a region.

A second *misconception* is that in those MENA countries that have developed lucrative oil exporting industries, the vast wealth brought in by oil has allowed society to proceed more easily through a rapid modernization process benefiting the whole population.

Each chapter in the book examined individual elements that affect women's status and, taken collectively, debunked these misconceptions. The MENA region does not present a homogeneous picture of women's status. Although the MENA region is first and foremost Islamic, women's status varies from one country to another based primarily on economic and political factors. Enforcement of Islamic laws is varied according to each government's needs and the political make-up of the country. Oil-producing countries, having created high paying jobs suitable for men, need and can afford to limit women's status to the familial role; there is no imperative to change. Non-oil-exporting MENA countries, by contrast, are less restrictive on women's entrance into the labor force and have created a better climate for women's social status to improve.

Furthermore, the sudden population boom in the MENA region (i.e., the youth bulge) experienced across the region threatens stability unless job creation can keep pace—another reason why governments have controlled women's status.

When examining the following selection of case studies, pay close attention to how each country has reached different degrees of social reality pertaining to women's status. It becomes clearer that while Islam is commonly portrayed as the main factor controlling women's lives and opportunities, the analysis in this study shows that there are other significant processes at work. I have selected MENA countries that differ from one another with respect to geography, economy, demographic and modernization characteristics (box 9.1), and cultural history. The six countries are Iran, Libya, Tunisia, Saudi Arabia, United Arab Emirates, and Yemen.

Box 9.1 Demographic characteristics of Iran, Libya, Tunisia, Saudi Arabia, United Arab Emirates, and Yemen.

Iran: Low fertility (2.0) and low maternal mortality (37), high FLFP relative to other MENA countries but still low (33 percent), 3 percent women in parliament

Libya: Medium level of fertility (3.9), low maternal mortality (75), FLFP (26 percent), 5 percent women as ministerial officials

Tunisia: Low fertility (2.1), low maternal mortality (70), FLFP (27 percent), 23 percent women in parliament, the highest in MENA region

Saudi Arabia: High fertility (5.7), low maternal mortality (23), FLFP (20 percent), zero participation of women in the parliament

UAE: Medium level of fertility (3.5), very low maternal mortality (3), zero participation of women in parliament

Yemen: High fertility (7.2), high maternal mortality (350), low FLFP (28 percent), zero participation of women in parliament

Source: Extracted from table 9.2.

Iran: Turbulence, Transition, and its Effects on Women's Social Status

Iran is included as a case study due to its cultural and political similarities, economic realities, and geographic proximity to the other oil-producing MENA countries. Today, for example, Iran along with Turkey and Saudi Arabia are the only MENA nations whose language and culture are synonymous with their national identity. In the rest of the MENA region, different population sectors within a country trace their heritage to one of many ancient civilizations or tribes. Under these circumstances, nationality is not necessarily connected to a person's ethnicity or culture.

In Iran, however, there are also important ethnic and historical differences that have caused the modernization process and resulting outcomes to deviate from what might have been predicted by existing models. An examination of Iran will reveal the forces that controlled and control the country, the outcomes and how they affect women's social status.

History presents Iran as a civilization with a continuous cultural identity spanning over twenty-five hundred years. Throughout history Iran has existed as an empire (superpower) and as conquered territory subject to foreign rule (Arabs, Turks, Mongols, British, Russians, to name a few). While the territorial domain of Iran has changed throughout the millennia, a unified people have always existed to exert a cultural identity unique to the rest of the world. The force of this individuality has allowed Iran to consistently reassert its national identity and develop into a distinct political and cultural entity. It is in Iran where, following Islamization during the eighth to tenth centuries, the combination of preexisting Iranian culture and the newly arrived Arab Sunni Islamic conversion yielded Shia Islam which, except for small pockets in other MENA countries, is a form of Islam considered unique to Iran and bordering regions.

Examining women's status in modern day Iran requires factoring in social forces and changes that took place starting in 1900. At the start of the twentieth century, Iran was neither a superpower nor did it have an oil-producing industry. Iran, however, was culturally ready for modernization. Petroleum was initially discovered in Iran during the first decade of the twentieth century.[1] By 1911, the Anglo-Persian Oil Company—APOC—was producing oil in Iran.

A major political change occurred in Iran in the 1920s with the imposition of a new prime minister on behalf of the military. Reza Shah, the new leader of Iran, was determined to modernize the country. Optimism about the chance for success was supported by the historical fact that Iran had once been a thriving empire. The development of the oil industry initiated the start of modernization in 1904 with a joint effort involving the British government. At that time,

> scholars estimate that Iran was one of the poorest nations in Asia. In a population of roughly 10 million in 1927, there were only 56,000 children in primary school, only 14,500 in secondary school, and only 600 in institutes of higher learning. Persia had only twenty modern manufacturing plants and about a thousand factory workers. (Pollack, 2004: 29)

With the rise of Reza Shah, the Russian presence in Iranian territory ended and relations with the United States and Great Britain were cultivated as future protection against Soviet intervention. In fact, Reza Shah and particularly his son Mohammad Reza Shah became loyal allies of the United States and Great Britain. It is important to point out how Iran, at the start of Reza Shah's modernization project, was an Islamic country, but like the Turkish leader Kemal Ataturk, Raza Shah wanted to build Iran on a model of secularization. He tried to hold religion separate from civil government. As modernization theory would predict, the influx of oil wealth led the state to build roads, railroads, telephone lines, and power plants. The legal system was revised based on the French model. Religious minorities were given protection while a system of state courts was set up to manage crime. Women's status improved slightly (mainly for elite women but not for less privileged ones) as gradually women and girls were admitted to newly established schools (see chapter six for details) and some limited jobs opened up for women in the labor market, mainly as teachers and secretaries. Public health care grew as a matter of investment while universities and medical schools were established. The tradition of veiled women was eliminated by laws prohibiting the veil, which created controversy, tension, and anger against Reza Shah's regime among the religious groups and religious elite.

Reza Shah's version of "secular" modernization had the anticipated effects on women's status. The industrialization, although based on a single product (oil), gave middle class and mainly urban women opportunities to finish high school and enter college if supported by their families. The revocation of veiling laws indicated a modernization process proceeding according to Western economic and social models (while ignoring local traditions and customs) due to the fact that the government and the majority religion existed as separate entities.

Although Iran quickly became the fifth largest oil producer in the world, the relationship with the developed nations deprived Iran of many profits that reduced the growth potential of the Shah's modernization project. Developed countries stepped in to provide the necessary industrial technology in exchange for control of the resources. By 1941, Reza Shah was replaced by his son Mohammad Reza Shah Pahlavi who was even a more pro-Western leader (and pro-modernization). He increased ties with European countries and the United States and accelerated the investment that would contribute to the modernization of the country and improvements in women's status. In 1963 Iranian women gained the right to vote and hold public office. The Family Protection Acts (FPA) of 1967, which were revised in 1975, altered the legalities of women's rights in the home. The FPA put all family disputes through the secular courts. It made some changes in divorce, marriage, and temporary marriage. Female literacy increased significantly in the ten years between the first and revised FPA. In 1966 female literacy was reported to be 18 percent and it doubled in 1976 (36 percent) (Yeganeh, 1993).

In 1975, under the Shah's regime, Iran's sanction of polygamy was revised limiting men to a second wife, conditional on the court's permission *and* the permission of the first wife.

The FPA that essentially retained the provisions of the early enactment of 1967 was revised in 1975 to raise the age of marriage from fifteen to eighteen for females and from eighteen to twenty for males (Joseph and Najmabadi, 2005; Mir-Hosseini, 1993). Women also gained more rights to petition for divorce, for example, a woman could initiate divorce if her husband married another woman without her consent (Joseph and Najmabadi, 2005). However, the tension between the religious elite and the modernizing Shahs is well recorded in Iranian history, and the tension continued until 1978 when the son of Reza Shah, Mohammad Reza Shah, the second king of the Pahlavi dynasty, was overturned by the Islamic government of Ayatollah Khomeini.

With the 1979 Islamist revolution, there was a major rollback of reformed family laws. With the pressure from the conservative religious elites, the Islamists revoked the FPA and rolled back the clock on the legal improvements that Iranian women had gained in 1975. Among the more outrageous changes was reducing the marriageable age of girls to nine years. (Joseph and Najmabadi, 2005). The Islamists also made veiling mandatory—another rollback and a demonstration of the government repressive attitude toward women and women's rights (Mir-Hosseini, 1993, 2000; Moghadam, 1994).

To see the results of Iran's modernization and the effects on women's status, as compared to a select group of countries, data show (table 9.2) that after the population growth that the country experienced beginning with the Islamic Revolution of 1979, the rate of natural increase has dropped to 1.2, second lowest only to Tunisia. Iran's fertility rate is the lowest in the group, at 2.0, with a low rate of maternal mortality (both indicators of modernization). Women have a small role in government with a 3 percent representation in parliament (in 2004), which is consistent with the effects of converting the secular government to a religious one based on historically patriarchal traditions. In spite of the patriarchal system imposed by the government, female educational attainment from 1985 to 2003 increased more than it had during the programs of the previous leader, Mohammad Reza Shah Pahlavi. Female enrollment during this period rose from 36 to 75 percent (table 9.2) with the university population being 47 percent female by 2000 (table 9.2). Among the six selected countries, women's employment in Iran is the highest with an income disparity of 28 percent compared to men (third highest of the group; table 9.2). Married women in Iran have the lowest rate of participation in the labor force compared to single and widowed women. Divorced women have the highest rate of participation in the labor force (Salehi-Isfahani, 2000).

As discussed in earlier chapters, family planning programs are highly politicized and governments play a crucial role in banning or promoting them. The institutionalization of an "ideology of female domesticity" or "housewifization" in Iran after the 1979 revolution encouraged pro-natalist ideology. Modern contraceptive methods were discouraged, abortion was banned, and contraceptive devices were removed from pharmacies and clinics (Moghadam, 1993). Between 1976 and 1986 the population increased by 3.9 percent and the total fertility rate was 5.6, which placed Iran among the fastest growing countries in the region. In 1986 about 50 percent of the population was under the age of fifteen. By the end of the 1980s, the unfavorable effects of population increase were felt on the economy, health care services, the educational system, and the workforce. The government, influenced by religious leaders, reconsidered its earlier pro-natalist policies that resulted in a drastic decline in fertility within a decade. Where does Iran's fertility stand today? With a TFR of 2, Iran has succeeded in reaching the lowest fertility rate in the Middle East region and has the lowest TFR in the developing world (Larsen, 2001; Roudi-Fahimi, 2002). Three-quarters of married women in Iran use contraception, which is the highest rate among Muslim countries and comparable to many Western nations including the United States. In 2002, TFR in the United States was 2.1 compared with 2.0 for Iran.

In short, it is important to note that despite the return of Islamic fundamentalism to Iran, there has been a significant drop in the overall fertility rate and continued improvement of women's educational achievement. Their rate of participation in politics and the labor force, however, have not improved.

Libya and Tunisia: Reduced Fertility, High Rate of Women's Employment, and their Improved Social Status

Libya

The examination of the historical, sociocultural, and demographic changes among the MENA countries reveals that there have been no countries in which modernization occurred along the same line as in the West. In some MENA countries, women's status changed little despite the sudden economic boom due to oil. In other countries, lacking the oil wealth, women's status sometimes improved and sometimes did not. Libya began developing a lucrative oil export industry in the 1960s. In 1969, a revolution had replaced the monarchy with a secular military ruler whose plans were to modernize the country. The Qadhafi government made a concerted effort to advance female emancipation (Metz, 1987). Women were considered a source of labor in an economy with a high demand for workers. Metz also suggests that the government was interested in increasing its political support by promoting women's rights. "Since independence, Libyan leaders have been committed to improving the condition of women but within the framework of Arabic and Islamic values. For this reason, the pace of change has been slow" (p. 27). Years of colonial rule by Italy and the modern mass media introduced new ideas resulting in new perceptions and practices. The development of the oil industry brought Western settlers and foreign workers who carried with them new ideas and values different from traditional Libyan culture. Social programs sponsored by the government (i.e., free health care, universal education) decreased the dependence of the elderly on their children in villages and even more so in the cities. For example, working mothers receive benefits that encourage them to continue working even after marriage and childbirth. A working woman can retire at age fifty-five and receive a state pension (Metz, 1987).

Different from all the other MENA countries examined, the changes enacted by the secular regime brought about by the 1969 revolution seem to have given modernization in Libya a flavor similar to what was experienced in the West. A significantly small percentage of Libyan women under age twenty-five are married (only 1 percent between fifteen and nineteen and 12 percent between twenty and twenty-four; table 9.2). The reason for the significant increase in age of marriage for Libyan women may find its explanation in the modernization theory. The interesting observation regarding Libya is that when it began its rapid industrialization process, it did so without a strong Islamic element present in the central government, but Islam was strong culturally. As a consequence, Islam is present in social traditions, but it did not serve as the blueprint for the country's economic and social development plans that were instituted when the country became prosperous with oil revenue.

With the rise in oil prices starting in the early 1970s, Libya's GDP grew dramatically. While Libya's oil production declined by half between 1970 and 1974, revenues from oil exports actually quadrupled. Libya's Five-Year Economic and Social Transformation Plan (1976–1980) added billions of dollars to the development of economic activities that would diversify its economy as a precaution to the anticipated end to the petroleum reserves (Metz, 1987). The agricultural sector received the most aid in an effort to make Libya self-sufficient in food and to help keep the rural population on the land. Industry received a significant amount of funding in the first development plan as well as in the second, launched in 1981. Oil revenue made possible a substantial improvement in the lives of virtually all Libyans. During the 1970s, the government succeeded in making major improvements in the general welfare of its citizens (Metz, 1987). The government passed a series of laws regulating female employment including the law requiring equal pay for equal work and qualifications. By the mid-1980s all students in secondary schools and above were drafted into military training. Women were also encouraged to attend military academies (Metz, 1987). Libya has an impressive 108 percent rate[2] for secondary school enrollment for both males and females. In sum, the diversification of Libya's process of modernization was a significant factor for women making inroads on the work and education fronts, but it did not reduce the importance of Islam in peoples lives.

Tunisia

Tunisia's geographic location, at the crossroads of the Mediterranean, Africa, and the Middle East and less than one hundred miles south of Europe, brought centuries of interactions and exchanges with the different tribes and peoples of Africa, the religion and traditions of the Middle East, and the culture of Europe. The last major cultural exchange came when Tunisia became a French Protectorate (colony) in 1881. Following World War II, Tunisia was the first of the European colonies in Africa to declare independence.

The influence of different cultures in Tunisia's history and its geographic proximity to a diverse world appear to have had an effect on women's status early in the nineteenth century. The Sadiki School in 1874, and the resulting reforms would alter the course of women's status and family law through the remainder of the millennium. The purpose for this school was to modernize the educational system in Tunisia to the point of equality with the academic achievements of Western civilization. Establishment for Sadiki School is a marker for the modernization process within Tunisian ideology, culture, and society. During French domination there was an active anticolonial movement that seems to have caused a natural attraction toward such Western ideas as democracy, freedom, and social justice. In 1910, student revolts against the French began and in an effort to grow the movement, women were allowed to attend schools and a free press was established (Simmons and Stone, 1976).[3]

Women's status improved further with Tunisia's independence from France. The first government of the independent nation, combined with a social ideology heavily influenced by foreign cultures, embarked on a mission to modernize the country using Western nations as models. While some of the European colonies, once they gained independence, fell into chaos and instability, often struggling between secular and religious direction, Tunisia's first independent government maintained state security while modernizing the country.

An examination of the data demonstrates the success of Tunisia in advancing women's status closer to that of men during the same time period in which other MENA countries, following a similar history, had very different results. Tunisia is considered one of the most progressive countries promoting gender equality in marital relations. The Family and Personal

Status Code applies to all citizens regardless of their religious affiliation. According to the Tunisian personal status code, a man cannot divorce his wife without grounds (repudiation is not accepted). The divorce has to be obtained through the courts and either spouse is entitled to compensation, especially when the divorce will impose a harmful financial and emotional outcome on one of the spouses. The care and well-being of any children in a marriage is the joint responsibility of both parents. In the case of a divorce, the court will determine custody, taking the children's best interest into account (Arab Human Development Report, 2005). When comparing the six countries cited in this chapter, Tunisia ranks number one for the percentage of female members of parliament. From 1995 to 2004 that number rose from 7 to 23 percent of the parliament. Total fertility Rate for Tunisia is 2.1, surpassed only by Iran (2.0). The data for average age of marriage also shows the effects of successful modernization. Among this group, Tunisia and Libya, where women's status has improved the most, have the least number of women getting married in the youngest age group of fifteen–nineteen (table 9.2). This would have been predicted by modernization theory. Although Tunisia lacks a significantly profitable oil industry, the female literacy rate, as a percentage of male literacy, is equal to the wealthier oil producing members of the MENA region. Almost half of the university enrollment in 2000 was made up of female students. Finally, Tunisian women earn salaries that on average are 36 percent of men's salaries. While it may seem low, it is the highest of the six countries in this comparative analysis.

However, in the two decades between 1980 and early-to-mid-2000, many countries experienced a dramatic jump in the enrollment of both male and female students in secondary school (table 9.2). For example, in 1985, 57 percent of women in Libya were enrolled in secondary school compared with 108 percent in year 2000. Oman and Tunisia provide other great examples; only 18 percent of girls in Oman and 32 percent in Tunisia were enrolled in secondary school in 1985. By the year 2000, 78 and 81 percent of girls were enrolled in Oman and Tunisia, respectively.

While Tunisian history may have been steeped in tradition and Islam, similar to other MENA countries, the diversity of ideologies introduced by a history of interaction with multiple outside cultures produced a more effective modernization process and greater improvement in women's status. Compared to the other countries, women's status was more easily redefined in the Tunisian socioeconomic context. As implied in previous chapters, a single model of modernization theory cannot be made to fit all countries equally. The inner logic of the Tunisian political system shows how the different bases on which nations are built has very different implications for status of women.

Saudi Arabia: The Heart of the Stasis of Tradition in the MENA Region

The analysis of the effects that oil wealth had and continues to have on Islam is a complex subject where political, military, religious, and cultural lines intersect. Saudi Arabia is the example of choice for an examination of how oil wealth has harnessed the power of Islam, and how Islam has harnessed the wealth gained from oil.

Saudi Arabia, the ancestral center of Islam, experienced an internal struggle with its Islamic identity. The Wahhabi reform movement of the eighteenth century fought to restore all laws and lifestyles to those established in the beginning of the Islamic era (800–950). They considered all changes to Islam, after 950, null and void. Expelled from Medina, Saudi Arabia, the founder of the Wahhabi sect, Muhammad ibn Abd al-Wahab, converted the Saud tribe to Wahhabism (Bowen, 2007). A holy war (jihad) ensued resulting in the conquest of neighboring tribes by 1763. By 1811 the Wahhabis ruled all of Arabia. Their power was lost due to the intervention of more powerful Egyptian forces and then by 1833 it was restored throughout the Persian peninsula (Algar, 2002).

The discovery of the massive oil reserves, with its vital importance to the West for both economic and military growth, represents the major source of revenue for Saudi Arabia's government. The ruling family and the oil industry control the nation's wealth, and the ruling family's fundamentalist Islamic beliefs control the population (particularly women who have no status) breeding an interdependence of petro-wealth and Islam. Petro-wealth has allowed Saudi Arabia, since its birth as a recognized nation in 1932, to expand its influence through the direct export of Wahhabism (Beinin and Stork, 1996; Encyclopedia of Islam and the Muslim World, 2004) (also see chapter one and the influence of Wahhabism in Saudi Arabia). Saudi Arabia, through direct foreign assistance, is able to exert political influence on other parts of the Islamic world. For example, the Saudi government, in its effort to spread the influence of Islam, finances the construction of Wahhabi schools and mosques in countries both in and outside the Islamic world.

Wahhabism has grown from an obscure sect to become mainstream Islamic teaching on all continents (see chapter one for more on Wahhabism). Wahhabist's influence became possible with the petro-wealth accumulated in the twentieth century. Their continued influence relies, and will continue to rely on the ability of the Saudi ruling family to control the population, which it has done, so far, through money and Islam (Algar, 2002; Beinin and Stork, 1996; Encyclopedia of Islam and the Muslim World, 2004).

Today's Saudi Arabia is a monarchy governed under the strict Islamic laws of the Wahhabi sect, which controls and regulates all public behavior. The country is divided into thirteen *emirates* or *manatiq* each ruled by a governor appointed by the king. The emirates are further divided into governorates. Saudi Arabia, perhaps, is the best example of a MENA society deeply rooted in tribal and patriarchal tradition. The unification of the tribal lands into the official Kingdom of Saudi Arabia was completed by Abdul Aziz ibn Saud in 1932. Modernization was expected to begin in the 1930s with the discovery and development of the largest oil fields in the world. This gave Saudi Arabia a strategic importance in World War II and transformed the Kingdom. While the oil revenues provided the ruling family with great wealth, their position as absolute monarchs and adherence to social tribal tradition meant the influx of oil revenue was not accompanied by a parallel social revolution and modern development as had occurred in some of the other oil-producing nations. The Saudi ruler is not subjected to any institutional limit, but only by the interpretation of the Quran. The attachment to tribal society was so strong that they once feared the rise of Arab Nationalism from Syria and Egypt.

In examining the foundation of modern Saudi Arabian social structure, we see, as with other MENA countries, a history of strict adherence to patriarchal rules reinforced by an equally strict interpretation of Islam. The initial formation of the Kingdom of Saudi Arabia had just begun when lucrative oil deposits were discovered and developed. Therefore we see a complex web of centuries of tradition that they sought to maintain, combined with oil wealth and a country they wanted to dramatically transform.

Formation of the modern Saudi Arabian nation took place with no separation between religion and state. In fact, the Wahhabi Islamic religion was used as the blueprint for a unified Saudi Arabia. While modern principles and technology were followed in developing the oil industry and conducting international business, social status continued along the same lines as it had for the previous millennium. The influx of wealth and the international importance given to its oil reserves did initiate a modernization process, but this was limited, as we have seen in other oil-producing MENA states, to infrastructure and industrial development. Saudi Arabia's population of natives is close to thirty million but with a rate of natural increase of 2.7 its population doubles every fifty years (table 9.2). About 30 percent of its population is foreign-born and over 60 percent of its labor force is foreign-born migrant workers (table 9.2). Female share of the labor force has been increasing for the past three decades from 5 percent in 1980 to 13 in the year 2000 but is still among the lowest in the region and in the world (table 9.2). Unemployment rate for women is among the highest in the region. Men's unemployment rate was 5.2 while women's was reported to be as high as 11.5 percent in the year 2000. Literacy rate is relatively high in Saudi Arabia, and women's enrollment in secondary schools and university is high as well (table 9.2).

Among the countries selected for this analysis, Saudi Arabia's current fertility rate of 5.7 is significantly higher than that other countries, surpassed only by Yemen. Mortality rates have been reduced making it second only to the United Arab Emirates. The rate of young female marriage, in the age group of fifteen–nineteen, is relatively low and the female literacy rate is the second highest of the select group members (the six countries elected in this chapter for the analysis). Among the countries we are comparing, Saudi Arabian women have the highest percentage of presence in university studies making up the majority of university students. While these modernization indicators are predictable, viewing the twentieth-century history of the country (unification to wealth accumulation through oil industry development), an analysis of other indicators shows the clear control of the pre-modernization patriarchal system. Although health care improvements have lowered mortality, and education attainment has risen to the point of having 56 percent of the university population made up by women, there is 0 percent of female participation in their parliament (similar to United Arab Emirates and Yemen). Female labor force participation is the lowest in the six select groups of countries with women earning only 20 percent of what men earn (table 9.2).

Further limiting the entrance of women into the labor force, and as a consequence, limiting any change in their social status, Saudi Arabia imports temporary migrant workers to fulfill its labor needs. This allows for the rapid modernization of the country via expendable foreign labor with no citizenship status, while eliminating the need to allow female labor force development. This is where it becomes apparent that the modernization process in MENA countries with strong historical roots in a patriarchal social tradition, which did not experience a separation of religion and state prior to industrialization, does not follow the same trajectory as that predicted by the Western models.

United Arab Emirates: High Rate of Labor Immigration and High Level of Female Education but Low Female Employment Rate

While countries such as Iran had thousands of years as a culturally rich expansive empire, and Tunisia interacted for millennia with cultures from three continents, the history of the United Arab Emirates is very different resulting in a different modern day reality for the social status of women. The United Arab Emirates lacked strategic importance until the discovery of oil in the twentieth century. Because the United Arab Emirates is historically a tribal society, kinship and tribal associations bring about most political and economic activity. While the discovery of oil and the increasing contact with the West has led to material and social changes, the period of modernization of the United Arab Emirates progressed with the culture firmly rooted in the traditional tribal traditions and strict Islamic rule. This is reflected in the way the government is structured. The UAE constitution, formalized in 1971, created a federation of seven emirates. Historically important tribes divided the power in the Supreme Council of the Union with one head of state chosen by the council. There are no political parties, which thus precludes the introduction of any progressive ideology. Foreign nations deal directly with each individual tribe in order to access the oil reserves located on tribal land—the inseparable union between religion and state lead to a hybrid modernization.

Changes in the economy and infrastructure increase wealth and quality of life while, at the same time, the historical patriarchy and social rules are preserved intact. Women are excluded from political leadership positions (0 percent female participation in parliament). Modernization had led to investment in health care technology, extended to both men and women, lowering maternal mortality more than the other six countries in the study group. Marriage of young women is low confirming what modernization theory would predict. Female educational attainment is very high also confirming the effects of modernization investment in education and promotion of female entrance into the school system.

However, the modernization process in the United Arab Emirates, with its improvements in female mortality and female education attainment, falls short of the expected results due to the control of political power by traditional tribal culture. Examining the economic status of women in the labor force, female income in the United Arab Emirates is, together with neighboring Saudi Arabia, at the bottom with women earning only 21 percent of salaries compared to men. As seen with other oil-producing MENA countries, the tendency is to import migrant workers, and prevent them from obtaining citizenship or establishing families. By the end of the twentieth century, 90 percent of the UAE labor force was foreign (table 9.2). By prohibiting citizenship and family rights to migrant workers, the United Arab Emirates is able to support its economy while precluding significant foreign influence and change introduced to native culture.[4]

In common with Saudi Arabia, the strong historical patriarchal tradition in the United Arab Emirates is reinforced by a strict form of Islam, which limits the modernization of women's status even while women enjoy the benefits of improved health care and education. No effects are seen with regards to improving their participation in the labor force or the political leadership of the country. Women's opportunities have remained within the realm of the home and family both before and during the modernization process.

Yemen: Experiencing the First Stage of Demographic Transition—High Fertility and Mortality

Unlike other cases of modernization, the timeline of societal evolution does not necessarily progress from tribal structure to national structure. In Yemen the existence of tribes and the state coexist. Yemeni tribes are territorial entities that were formed and solidified centuries before the concept of the state arrived in the area. As a result, the modern nation of Yemen is actually an agreed upon cooperation of the tribes who, in spite of a central national government and constitution, still exert control over tribal populations (Koury and Kostiner, 1991). Tribal culture persisted through the occupation of part of the southern land by the British in 1839, and control of the north by the Ottoman Empire. In 1918 North Yemen won independence from the Ottoman Empire and became a republic in 1962. In 1967 the British withdrew and the two areas eventually united as the Republic of Yemen in 1990 (Enders, 2001). Although Yemen may share borders and historical culture with its neighbor Saudi Arabia, its scarce oil reserves have altered the course of modernization in this country. Oil currently represents 90 percent of Yemen's export revenue. However it is predicted that the reserves fast disappearing. The amount of revenue brought in by exporting oil has not reached the same level of benefit as it has, and continues to have, in Saudi Arabia. As a result, Yemen can be viewed, through the model of dependency theory, as the secondary party dependent on the modernization of Saudi Arabia. Yemen's economy became dependent on exporting temporary labor to the wealthier GCC oil-producing nations. This brought in remittances that were critical to the national economy, but it failed to modernize Yemen to the point of becoming a self-sustaining economy. Yemen has yet to achieve a modernization of infrastructure and social status. With women's status controlled for millennia by a tribal-patriarchal system, the lack of economic and industrial development due to the lack of resources translates into a lack of momentum and reason for any change in women's status. As seen in the previous chapters (on women's work and references to the modernization process in the West), economic growth and prosperity can create a powerful need to bring women into the labor force. In Yemen, we see that the lack of economic growth and dependency on more developed nations can inhibit this change in women's status. Instability in Yemen prevents social change. For example, in 1990 approximately 850,000 Yemenis from the Persian Gulf states returned home (loss of remittances) while foreign aid was significantly reduced. By 1994 a civil war hampered economic growth and, by consequence, social change was unnecessary. While it is clear that none of the results of modernization process are visible in present day Yemen, we do see the clear consequences of dependency theory and how the end result, for women's status, is a lack of change.

A contrast of the demographic data in tables 9.2 positions Yemen at the bottom of the six selected countries we chose to compare. The rate of natural population increase is the highest as is the predicted population change by 2050. For a country showing a failed modernization process and strong dependency on the prosperity of its neighbors, the projected increases in population are alarming when compared to the other members of the group. This emphasizes the inability of women to control their own fertility. Energy use per capita and GNI PPP per capita (indicators of modernization) are significantly less than the other nations (oil-producing and non-oil-producing) in the

MENA region. In Yemen, women's participation in parliament is zero, equal to the situation in Saudi Arabia and the United Arab Emirates. Yemen also presents the highest percentage of young brides and lowest percentage of women using contraception (table 9.2). Educational attainment of women is also the lowest of the group as Yemen presents the highest percentage of female illiteracy (table 9.2).

DISCUSSION

The way many MENA countries deal with women's issues, placing an emphasis on traditionalism in the name of Islam, has often been a political strategy for these nations to deflect attention from their economic failures, high inflation rate, lack of ability to provide employment for everyone, and lack of adequate social services (Hijab, 1988; Moghadam, 1992b, 2004; Obermeyer, 1992). Experiencing rapid population growth (as high as 3–4 percent growth rate) and high male and female unemployment, many of the MENA countries adopted Islamization of the state and embraced traditional gender roles. Religious ideology, cultural beliefs, and traditional principles cannot be argued to be the one and only reason for women's status lagging behind in these countries. Countries such as Saudi Arabia, as one of the top oil producers of the world, did not require female labor in order to grow and develop economically (in a form of capital-intensive industry). In the oil-rich countries, the government hires foreign labor, which has become a permanent practice in those countries and is a crucial part of the fabric of their industrialization and modernization.

By contrast, countries such as Indonesia and Tunisia (no oil, majority Muslim) developed their economy through labor-intensive industrial production, took advantage of their female labor and therefore are characterized by a higher rate of female labor force participation and women's political participation and higher status of women (Ross, 2008).

The intent of this book was to analyze multiple aspects that have affected women's status in the MENA region—factoring in historical, cultural, religious, economic, and political forces responsible for changes or the lack thereof. The view of the MENA as a region experiencing a high population growth without a parallel growth in job creation may lead the reader to a pessimistic view of the future for the MENA region. This assumption, however, is not necessarily correct.

Studies of the modernization process have shown that women's status improves when they become essential to the financial system; when the unstoppable forces of a growing and a diversified economy are able to provide jobs at least equal to the demand. The data for educational attainment by women in MENA show the effects of modernization as in recent decades, the percentage women enrolled in higher education (university) has increased significantly. Some MENA countries present the majority of university students as female. According to Gary Becker (1991), this is indicative of a country's shift from underdeveloped to developed. The family dynamics change from having many children to provide labor for the parents, to smaller families where the parents invest more in the children through education (quantity versus quality). In the latter case, in the developed society, there is a greater return when parents invest in a smaller number of children. Society also benefits from a more educated and smaller population.

The future of women's status in MENA is dependent on the next course of modernization. The solution to the future improvement in women's status, as well as stabilization to the MENA region, can be derived from our case studies. In spite of great wealth, MENA countries that are dependent on a single industry (oil) actually suffered an incomplete modernization to the detriment of women. Political and economic status quo is maintained by reinforcing historically patriarchal ideologies. This however has not necessarily led to political stability and prosperity.

Improvement in the quality of life for people in the MENA region, and as a consequence, improvement in women's status, will occur if the current trajectory of the modernization process is altered according to observations taken from the Western modernization process. This theme is reflected in the studies by Salehi-Isfahani (2000). Although his discussion is centered on the size and distribution of population in Iran, and the effects this will have on economic and social development in the next few decades, his reasoning is applicable to all MENA countries experiencing a "youth bulge."

Salehi-Isfahani (2000) points out how in Iran, the 1979 revolution against the government was born among the disenfranchised youth. Following the revolution, Iran's fertility rate increased dramatically thus producing another, even larger, youth bulge. Hope, according to Salehi-Isfahani, lies in the government changing the country's base of economic growth from oil, to "human capital."[5] The oil industry, based on a finite quantity of a natural resource, produced a financial windfall for the Iranian economy—not a sustainable economic model. This is also true for the other major oil-producing nations such as Saudi Arabia, Kuwait, and the United Arab Emirates. Wherever there is a tight relationship between per capita income and oil exports, further complicated by rapid population growth, social and political scientists will see the potential for civil unrest and instability. And it is clear that an oil export based economy can have adverse effects on women's status.

The population boom seen across the MENA region in the 1970s and 1980s, followed by the rapid decline in fertility rates, can represent a danger to an oil based economy or a valuable asset to an economy in expansion. Throughout the MENA region, a youth bulge followed by a decline in fertility means that over time, the ratio of adults to children changes to produce more teachers/nurturers to raise fewer children. This facilitates the transition of economic growth away from oil and more toward human capital.

The timing of this transition is paramount. All the MENA countries with declining fertility rates must make a rapid investment in their human capital and create a diversified economic base for sustainable growth before the current youth bulge reaches retirement (estimated around 2040). At that point there will be a smaller cohort of working contributors to care for a larger elderly population. Investment in human capital today, and diversification of a sustainable economy away from just an oil based industry, will provide tomorrow's generations with stability and prosperity.

Women's social status in the MENA countries has been and continues to be conditioned by the economic and political realties of the region. When expedient, Islam and historical traditions of patriarchy have been engaged as frameworks and justifications for controlling the population. However, in Islamic countries where we see a more diversified economy, Islam has not been an altogether limiting influence. Therefore, we can predict a substantial improvement in the future of women's status in MENA region if it is able to move away from the reliance on oil exports and focus on an investment in human capital and a diversified economy with ample jobs. With the population growth under control, and women already achieving higher educational attainment, regional stability and prosperity lies in continued and intelligent modernization. Most importantly, women's status would improve by virtue of the natural economic forces that would ensue from stability and economic diversification.

NOTES

1 INTRODUCTION

1. The debate lies in the notion that the geographic position of the region is considered the "Middle East" to Europeans and Americans only but to other countries "Middle East" is not located in the East of their region. For example, to China the region is not the "Middle East" and is positioned to the west of it.

2. "Orientalism" was coined with the publication of Edward Said's scholarly work and is responsible for a growing body of literature in the humanities and social sciences. It originated from Michel Foucault's thesis on the relationship between power and knowledge in popular and scholarly thinking. He notes that the Western world constructed a false and "untrue" image of "Eastern" societies based on facts and on preconceived notions that Eastern societies are backward, culturally, political, and intellectually inferior, and not equal to the "West." He argued that this notion is rooted in the Eurocentric view and dates back to the time of colonialism and Western imperialism.

3. The World Bank refers to this category as "lower middle income economies."

4. The concept of *Sharm* has no equivalent in English. The closest translation is a combination of the words shame, charm, and modesty, which are considered central to a woman's desirability and inner and outer beauty in many traditional Muslim, Hindu, orthodox Jewish, and traditional Christian communities. Family virtue and honor is directly related to the ability of men to control their family through women's modesty in dress and in behavior.

5. The concept of *Fatwa* means the interpretation of difficult questions about Islam, particularly questions and issues that are not addressed in the present day legal/law system. In the Muslim world, only the highest levels of Islamic leaders (i.e., Ayatollah

Rouhollah Khomeini of Iran) have the religious authority to
issue a *Fatwa*.

6. Cotter et al. (2004: 1) in their report titled *Gender Inequality at Work* state: "Labor force participation is often seen as the prime indicator (and cause) of changes in women's status. As far back as Frederich Engels' or Charlotte Perkins Gilman's writing on the subject in the late 1800s, social scientists and other observers have identified employment outside the home as the starting point for understanding women's position in society. Social theory often focuses on women's employment because employment determines their access to resources and their ability to make independent decisions."

2   THE MODERNIZATION THEORY

1. In the early stages of development, women's withdrawal from the labor force is caused by (i) the improvement of men's wages and the growth of the middle class status (the "wealth effect"), and (ii) separation of workplace and home, location of work changes from the home domain and agriculture to the outside of the home in a different location (e.g., office setting or factory). This separation is usually accompanied by an inflexible work schedule. Thus, these limitations result in the reduction of female employment outside the home due to household and child care responsibilities.

2. Daniel Bell's classical description (1999) of the postindustrial society is one where its main feature is the growth of service occupations, mainly blue-collar and lower level white-collar jobs that are primarily producing goods and services. The higher level white-collar and managerial occupations (engineers, computer scientists, scientists, and professionals of all kinds) are in charge of information and knowledge production. Therefore a postindustrial society's main focus of production is on goods, services, and knowledge.

3. This perspective is sometimes referred to as the neoclassical perspective.

3   THE GLOBAL ECONOMY

1. Smith (2005), for example, proposes a reason for gender inequality in Latin America as religious based and thus similar to the explanation for the Middle East as it has been proposed by some researchers. The differences lie not in the religion dictating the

role of women, but in the fact that in Catholic Latin America the women tend to identify with the figure of the Virgin Mary (Smith, 2005). Smith uses the coined terms of "marianismo" and "supermadre" used to label women's values in opposition to the men's role as subscribed to "machismo." Women's influence in the family and society stem from the Roman Catholic Church's definition of womanhood and motherhood being the embodiment of the nature of the Virgin Mary who represented the highest form of female behavior. The indirect result of the church teachings is a patriarchal society. The domain of Latin American women is the home while the domain of Latin American men is the public arena.

2. Other studies have been conducted by Black and Cottrell (1981); Iglitzen and Ross (1986); Joakes (1987); Malhotra et al. (1995); Marshal (1985); Moghadam (1988); O'Kelly and Carney (1985); Patai (1967); Young (1988).

3. Dependent capitalism is explained by dependency theory (see section on dependency theory later in this chapter). Dependent capitalism is the concept that economically underdeveloped nations, despite their role in the global economy and rapid economic growth, do not experience the same achievements or standard of living present in economically developed nations. This is attributed to the relationship between the underdeveloped and developed countries, a relationship in which the resources of the underdeveloped country is exploited or purchased and then transformed into capital, which accumulates in the developed country. The result is that underdeveloped countries, dependent on developed capitalist countries, never go through the same social and political processes and therefore never "catch up" with the developed world (Bossen, 1984).

4. See later in this chapter and the following chapters for an explanation of how women's right to enter the workforce can impact the economic stability of the country by raising unemployment and the need for state funded social services to replace women who leave the home.

5. As we discussed earlier the Middle East was first subjugated by European colonial powers whose sole interest was economic exploitation of natural resources and cheap local labor needed to harness those resources. Following the end of European colonialism, a type of economic control through the arrival of transnational corporations (i.e., the start of the global economy) began. For example, in the first four decades of the

Anglo-Iranian Oil Company (AIOC), the division of profits for Iranian oil was 93 percent in favor of England with the remaining 7 percent going to Iran (Tertzakian, 2006). Initially the cooperation between the developed (United Kingdom) and the developing worlds (Iran) added wealth and jobs to the Iranian economy (Tertzakian, 2006). However within one generation it was evident that other than exploitation of petroleum as a natural resource, cheap labor in Iran to extract the oil was being exploited to increase foreign profits when the refined fuels were sold internationally. Iran demanded a 50–50 division of the profits, which was refused by England. The result was an attempt in 1951 to nationalize the Iranian oil industry, which was defeated. Powers of the developed world eventually regained control and divided Iranian oil profits (40 percent England, 40 United States, and 20 Iran). The resentment of exploitation continued until the advent of the Islamic Revolution in 1979, which restored control of Iranian natural resources to the Iranian government (p. 71).

6. There are two sides to women's marginalization in the international division of labor: (i) On the demand side, labor-intensive industries such as garment, electronics, and food production often prefer to hire young women since they are perceived as docile, reliable, and easier to exploit (Cho and Koo, 1983; Fernandez-Kelly, 1983; Safa, 1983). Therefore, multinational corporations take advantage of inexpensive and available labor and prefer women to men. (ii) On the supply side, women's wages become an important contribution to the survival of the family. Lower class women become more active in the labor force but as a form of exploited labor and much to their disadvantage (Cho and Koo, 1983; Wallerstein, 1984; Ward, 1984). For example, Beneria and Sen (1982, 1986) argue that economic marginalization of women in the process of development is a result of exploitation of their labor in the global capitalist labor relation system.

5   Women's Status And Fertility Patterns

1. The demographic transition model (DTM): The demographic changes in a society from high birth and death rates to low birth and death rates are considered to be part of the economic development of a country, where the changes involve the transformation from a preindustrial to an industrialized economy. The

change in the population that occurs over time is often referred
as the DTM. The general description of the model is as follows:

- In the preindustrial stage both birth and death rates are high
  and there is very little population growth. Historical docu-
  ments indicate that during some periods in history, population
  declined instead of staying stable or slightly increasing. For
  example, during both the sixth and the fourteenth centuries,
  Europe experienced plagues that drastically reduced its population by 40 percent (Russell, 1958: 41). Industrialization
  in Europe meant that more men and women could marry
  younger because of the availability of jobs outside of the agricultural sector. Men could afford to support a family by taking on jobs instead of depending on parents for farm work
  and land inheritance. Weller and Bouvier (1981) state: "As
  urbanization and industrialization took place, the family lost
  importance as an economic unit of production. Industrial
  systems like the factory took over the allocation of jobs. The
  occupational structure shifted away from primary industries
  such as agriculture (associated with high fertility levels) and
  toward white-collar and skilled industries (associated with
  lower fertility). Children who were useful as a cheap supply
  of labor in farming families were not as useful in industrial
  working-class families, particularly when child labor was
  abolished and compulsory education laws were passed. In
  fact, children began to be financial burdens as the costs of
  child rearing increased" (p. 28).
- As fertility rates continued to stay high, death rates dropped
  in record numbers. In European countries, mortality began
  to decline around the early nineteenth century, first slowly
  and then in an accelerated manner. The decline in mortality was a direct result of higher standards of living that was
  accompanied by industrialization. These standards were due
  to causes such as higher supply of food due to improvements
  in agricultural techniques, better and faster distribution of
  food, improvements in medical practices, sanitary reform, and
  public health awareness. Thus, it was not until the beginning
  of the twentieth century that medical practices and change in
  lifestyle made a significant impact on people's quality of life
  (McKeown, 1976).
- The third stage of the DTM is characterized by low fertility
  and mortality rates where mortality rates reach their lowest

and fertility rates can fluctuate moderately from one year to another. Population growth is steady but if there is any growth, it is due to fluctuating fertility and in-migration. Many of the Western countries had reached this stage for the past several decades. The population could actually decrease if the patterns of fertility and mortality persist unless they are offset by in-migration, as is the case in Canada and the United States.

The DTM is subject to debate. Oftentimes it does not apply to certain developing countries' population patterns where fertility stays high despite modernization, or unexpectedly drops (Coale, 1974; Kirk, 1971; Notestein et al., 1969: 144–145).

2. In the early stages of development, women's withdrawal from the labor force is caused by (i) an improvement in the earnings of male breadwinners and the growth of the middle class status (the "wealth effect") and (ii) separation of workplace and home (i.e., the relocation of work from the home domain and agriculture to the outside of the home in a different location, such as offices or factories). This separation is usually accompanied by inflexible work schedules. Thus, these limitations result in decline of female employment outside the home due to household and child care responsibilities (women's primary responsibilities; Anker and Hein, 1986; Boserup, 1970; Oakley, 1974; Ryan, 1975; Tilly and Scott, 1978).

3. The phenomenon of women getting married at an early age is also associated with poverty and rural residency. In Afghanistan and Bangladesh, for example (two South Asian primarily rural and low income Muslim countries), about half the females are married by age eighteen (54 and 51 percent, respectively; UNIFEM, 2004). And yet, the Western Asia/North Africa region (15 percent), South America (16 percent), and the former Soviet Asia have a smaller proportion of their women marry early (between the ages of fifteen and nineteen) compared with other regions such as West and Middle Africa (38 percent) and South Central/South East Asia (32 percent), where the greatest proportion of women are married at younger ages. Thus the relative high fertility in the region is not directly related to early marriage (UNIFEM, 2004).

4. Growth in urbanization has been argued to encourage less traditional values, less influence of kin members who control choice of spouses and timing of marriage, and therefore is associated

with a delay in marriage (Singh and Samara, 1996). Other studies show no association between increase in urbanization and delay in marriage (Mensch et al., 2005).

5. Yemen is the least economically developed country in the MENA region where about half of its population lives below US$ 2/day.

6. Yemen with high fertility and high mortality illustrates characteristics of a country in the first stage of demographic transition. See note 1 for further explanation of different stages of demographic transition theory.

6 EDUCATION AND STATUS OF WOMEN

1. Daniel Bell's classic analysis (1973, 1999) of postindustrial societies describes the preindustrial countries as "societies based on extracting their livelihood from agriculture, mining, fishing, timber, natural gas, or oil." Industrial societies are based on coordination and "fabrication of labor, energy, and machine technology for the manufacture of goods." Finally, a postindustrial society's livelihood is based on processing of knowledge and information: "Telecommunications and computers are strategic for the exchange of information and knowledge" (Bills, 2004: 84).

2. Proximate determinants or intermediate variables of fertility were first introduced by Davis and Blake (1956) and it has been used extensively by demographers, public health experts, economists, and sociologists to explain fertility patterns in different countries. It is an analytic framework for understanding causes of fertility reduction or increase. Davis and Blake argued that any social factor influencing changes in fertility level of a society has to work through the eleven intermediate variables that are placed into three distinct groups. They listed the three groups as (i) exposure to sexual intercourse, (ii) risk of conception, and (iii) likelihood of live birth. Background factors such as educational attainment of a person works in conjunction with intermediate variables of fertility to reduce or increase fertility.

3. The larger gap remains in rural areas.

4. The fact that 108 percent of women are enrolled in secondary school needs clarification. Normally this data would come from the number of women enrolled in secondary school divided by the number of women of secondary school age (maximum = 100 percent). However, since we have added women outside the secondary school age group who have reentered the secondary

school system to further their education, we have a numerator greater than the denominator which results in a greater than 100 percent attendance.

5. The Gulf monarchies are also known as the Arabian Monarchies of the Persian Gulf, the Gulf Cooperation Council, or GCC states. The six countries that are part of the GCC Council are Bahrain, Oman, Qatar, Saudi Arabia, Kuwait, and United Arab Emirates.

6. There are three important elements effecting the recovery and growth of MENA economies directly tied to any improvement in women's status (including employment)—global prices for food and feed grains increased more than 50 percent during the first half of 2008 while oil revenues have fluctuated drastically upward and downward due to changes in demand and the world economy (World Bank, 2009). The continued expansion of population in the MENA region, albeit at a constantly slowing rate, has increased domestic demand in several economies (notably Egypt, the Islamic Republic of Iran, and a number of GCC countries). This has led to a sharp rise in consumer price inflation across the MENA region. The World Bank reports two temporary measures being taken in the region to alleviate the effects of inflation. Some countries have increased fuel and food subsidies while others have increased salaries. However, in the absence of true economic growth, these measures are counterproductive. They do not effectively manage inflation and further limit the government's resources to expand the economy to achieve permanent solutions (The World Bank, 2009).

7 DEFINITION AND PATTERNS

1. Words commonly associated with "work" are: employment, paid/ unpaid work, waged/unwaged work, paid/unpaid labor, occupation, job, labor force participation, reproductive labor, market/ nonmarket contribution of work, economic activity status, work in the formal/informal sector, economically productive activity.

Definitions of Rates and Concepts Related to "Work":

Employment rate—number of employed people (men or women) relative to the total population of working age (often between ages of 15–65).

The participation or activity rate—number of reported employed people added to the number of registered unemployed people of working age.

Female share of the labor force—share of women's participation in the labor force as the percent of the total (employed women relative to employed total).

Female labor force participation—percent of women in the labor force as the percent of the rest of the women between working age (employed women relative to other women).

PART TIME JOBS:
The International Labor Office (ILO) defines part-time jobs as those involving a significantly lower number of hours than the normal hours worked (Hussmans et al., 1990), whereas the Organization for Economic Cooperation and Development (OECD) defines part-time work as usual working hours fewer than 30 hours per week. Hakim (1993, 1997) lists three types of part time jobs:

Reduced hours—defined as weekly hours, close to the normally expected full time hours (for example, 30 hours instead of 37 hours—common in Sweden, Denmark, Norway.

Half-time jobs (15–29 hours a week)—common in Britain, Germany, France and Belgium.

Marginal jobs (only a few hours a week)—common in the Netherlands.
Hakim (2004) reports that most women in the U.S., Greece, Spain, and Portugal work full time. Also in Eastern Europe, part time work did not exist before the political upheavals and it is still not the most common type of work for women in those countries (Van der Lippe and Dijk, 2002).

2. In the early stages of development, women's withdrawal from the labor force is caused by (i) the improvement of earnings of men's wages and the growth of the middle class status (the "wealth effect") and (ii) separation of workplace and home, location of work changes from the home domain and agriculture to the outside of the home in a different location (e.g., office setting or factory). This separation is usually accompanied by an inflexible work schedule. Thus, these limitations result in the reduction of female employment outside the home due to household and child care responsibilities.

3. Different tiers of women are exploited in the global market economy and international division of labor even further. For example, Parrenas (2000), in her study of Filipina domestic workers, describes the formation of a "three-tier transfer of reproductive labor." She points to different tiers as the following: (1) The first tier consists of middle class women in receiving nations, who often benefit from immigrant women's labor. (2) The second tier consists of the migrant domestic workers who leave behind their own families and perform domestic labor for middle class women in the receiving nations. (3) The third tier is made up of the "third world" women from the lower classes who are too poor to migrate, and who oftentimes might end up caring for the families of the ones who left their families behind or are employed in extremely low paid jobs.

8 LABOR MIGRATION AND OIL REVENUE

1. During the 1970s, oil-producing countries blossomed and gained overnight economic success, while for countries importing oil this was an alarming economic and political era. Debeir et al. (1991) state that:

> The 1973–74 oil crisis had its roots in the long period of cheap energy in the preceding quarter of a century; it was also a by-product of the general political and economic conjuncture of capitalist worlds; finally and most importantly, it highlighted a fundamental structural phenomenon on which the whole capitalist growth of the 20th century had been based: the systematic depletion of fossil fuels. (P. 136)2.

2. The six Gulf Cooperation Council (GCC) countries are Saudi Arabia, Kuwait, Bahrain, Qatar, United Arab Emirates, and Oman. All are located on the Arabian Peninsula. Although Yemen is also located on the Arabian Peninsula, it is not included in this group.

3. For centuries, and up until the 1960s, slavery was practiced in the Middle East. Slaves were bought and sold at the slave markets all over the region. The practice was not unique to Muslims in the region but to Christians and Jews as well (Lewis, 1992). The large and continuous flow of voluntary labor migration started in the 1970s, due to the plummeting oil wealth. Slavery was abolished in the 1950s and 1960s in the entire region.

4. "Emigration" is the process by which people leave a country to settle in another while "immigration" is the movement of people into a country to settle. The United Nations defines

a "migrant" as a person who has been outside her country of birth or citizenship for twelve months or longer (regardless of legal status or any other reason).

5. The term originated in the 1970s in reference to the decline of manufacturing in Holland as a result of the discovery of massive natural gas reserves in the North Sea and the development of the Dutch Oil Companies.

9   CONCLUSION

1. Oil was discovered next in Iraq after World War I, in Bahrain in 1932 and in Saudi Arabia in 1933. World War II intervened and delayed the discovery of petroleum in other parts of the region. Since the 1950s, most of the oil-producing nations have become less technologically and politically dependent on British and American oil companies and they have accumulated wealth for the elite families and their governments (U.S. Library of Congress Country Studies).

2. The fact that 108 percent of women are enrolled in secondary school needs clarification. Normally this data would come from the number of women enrolled in secondary school divided by the number of women of secondary school age (maximum = 100 percent). However, since we have added women outside the secondary school age group who have reentered the secondary school system to further their education, we have a numerator greater than the denominator, which results in a greater than 100 percent attendance.

3. *Role of Sadiki School in Modern Tunisian Politics:* In the 1930s in Tunisia, while still under French colonial rule, the ruling Destour party was replaced by the Neo-Destour whose support was based in the rural areas. The Neo-Destour party, different from its predecessors, was founded by a new *intelligentsia* with foreign educational influence derived, in part, from graduates of the Sadiki College (or school) (founded by the Islamic reformer, Khaireddine, *prime minister of Tunisia* from 1873 to 1877). Important for the upcoming phase of modernization, the Sadiki College was designed around Western educational values that were intended to prepare Tunisia to compete with the European powers. Sadiki College, especially under the Neo-Destour, served as a conduit providing students from rural areas with access to the world of the elite. The curriculum included the study of French and promoted an understanding of the colonial administration. The school's graduates often continued their

education in France, which offered them exposure to political ideas that were both progressive and liberal. Simply put, the Neo-Destour party's mission was to achieve modernization through intellect while representing both the rural and urban populations. In contrast to Tunisia, other MENA countries proceeded with modernization within the framework of a strict religious framework, and/or by concentrating political power in a small group of monarchs/tribes. The Sadiki School helped bridge the gap between the urban elite and rural society by requiring education and intellect, and not social class to determine who participates. While scholars may point out that even with the Neo-Destour, there was a single party monopoly in Tunisia, it is more important to recognize how the government progressed toward modernization by "maintaining national cohesion and mobilizing the people along national and modernist lines while exercising a minimum of constraint and allowing a reasonable amount of discussion" (Micaud, 1964: xii). By unifying and mobilizing both the rural and urban populations prior to modernization, the government was better able to use education to transform values and social structures. As we have seen before when we examined countries experiencing modernization in the context of strong historical ties to patriarchy, Tunisia lacked this patriarchal tie. Neo-Destour first replaced the previous urban administrators (the religious leadership or ulema; the religio-judicial leadership, or muftis, caids and aduls, prominent merchants) and embraced Western ideas and technology to begin a modernization modeled on the political and economic realities facing all the people.

The pivotal role of rural mobilization for political stability in the developing world was the key to the success of this process (Huntington, 1968). Governments of developing countries (or what Huntington termed changing societies) that have rural support are better able to withstand the widespread instability engendered by economic development and the socioeconomic changes of modernization (pp. 433–461). In an analysis that emphasized social control in order for political institutions to develop, Huntington viewed the countryside as the source for political stability. The combination of rural majority and urban growth in the Third World gives rise to a distinctive pattern of politics in modernizing countries (King, 1998). As emphasized in other political theories, conflict can arise between urban and rural populations due to the different political attitudes resulting in opposition to the government. For modernization to be successful, political unity and stability is necessary as the Tunisian case had witnessed.

4. As explained earlier (chapter eight), in- and out-migration happens on a large scale in the MENA region. Many of the immigrants, depending on their skill level, personal choice, and availability of opportunities, often end up in the oil-producing nations, while a large number also immigrate to North American and European countries. Immigrants from Lebanon make up the highest percentage of the total labor force in the MENA countries (15 percent), followed by Morocco (7.6 percent), Tunisia (5.4 percent), and Algeria (4.5 percent). Immigrants from the MENA region hold disparate levels of education and skills. A majority of immigrants from Algeria (76.7 percent), Tunisia (73 percent), and Morocco (76.6 percent) entering the Organization for Economic Cooperation and Development (OECD) countries are low-skilled laborers (chapter eight). In contrast, most of the immigrants entering OECD countries that come from Qatar (69.6 percent), the United Arab Emirates (67.3 percent), Kuwait (67.8 percent), Saudi Arabia (65 percent), Oman (63 percent), Egypt (59 percent), Iran (59 percent), Jordan (56 percent), and Libya (54 percent) are reported to be high-skilled workers. This pattern reflects job opportunities for lower-skilled workers in oil-producing countries (absorbed by immigrant workers), but a shortage of job opportunities for more educated natives.

5. Human capital is often explained as the accumulation of knowledge and skill, embodied in an individual as a result of education, training, and experience, which makes the person more productive and more desirable in the job market and augments his or her contributions to the economy.

BIBLIOGRAPHY

Abdeljalil, Akkario. 2004. "Education in the Middle East and North Africa: The Current Situation and Future Challenges." *International Education Journal*, 5:2, 144–153

Abraham-Van Der Mark, E. 1983. "The Impact of Industrialization on Women: A Caribbean Case." *Women, Men and the International Division of Labor*. Eds. J. Nash and M.P. Fernandez-Kelly. Albany: State University of New York Press, pp. 823–838.

Abu Khalil, As' ad. 1993. "Toward the Study of Women and Politics in the Arab World: The Debate and the Reality." *Feminist Issues*, 13:1 (Spring), 3–22.

Adams, Richard H., Jr. "Migration, Remittances and Development: The Critical Nexus in the Middle East and North Africa." UN/POP.EGM/2006/01, April 18, 2006. United Nation expert group meeting on international migration and development in the Arab region. Population Division, Department of Economic and Social Affairs. Beirut, May 15–17, 2006. Retrieved on August 10, 2006, http://www.un.org/esa/population/publications/EGM_Ittmig_Arab/P01_Adams.pdf.

Afonja, S. 1981. "Changing Modes of Production and the Sexual Division of Labor among the Yoruba." *Signs: Journal of Women in Culture and Society*, 7, 299–313.

Ahmed, Leila. 1992. *Women and Gender in Islam: Historical Roots of a Modern Debate*. New Haven: Yale University Press.

Algar, Hamid. 2002. *Wahhabism: A Critical Essay*. Oneonta, NY: Islamic Publications International.

Ali, Kamran Asdar. 1997. "Modernization and Family Planning Programs in Egypt." *Middle East Report*, 205 (December), 40–44.

———. 2002. *Planning the Family in Egypt: New Bodies, New Selves*. Austin: University of Texas Press.

Al-Lail, Haifa R. Jamal. 1996. "Muslim Women between Tradition and Modernity: The Islamic Perspective." *Journal of Muslim Minority Affairs*, 16:1 (January), 99–110.

Altorki, S. 1986. *Women in Saudi Arabia. Ideology and Behavior Among the Elite*. New York: Columbia University Press.

Alwin, Duane, Michael Braun, and Jacqueline Scott. 1992. "The Separation of Work and the Family: Attitudes towards Women's Labor-Force Participation in Germany, Great Britain, and the United States." *European Sociological Review*, 8, 13–37.

Amin, Sajeda, Ian Diamond, Ruchira T. Naved, and Margarent Newby. 1998. "Transition to Adulthood of Female Garment-Factory Workers in Bangladesh." *Studies in Family Planning*, 29 (June), 185–200.

Amin, Samir. 1974. *Accumulation on a World Scale*. New York: Monthly Review Press.

———. 1997. *Capitalism in the Age of Globalization*. London: Zed Books.

Anker, Richard. 1998. *Gender and Jobs Sex Segregation of Occupations in the World*. Geneva: International Labour Office.

———. 2001. "Theories of Occupational Segregation by Sex: An Overview." *Women, Gender and Work*. Eds. Martha F. Loutfi. Geneva: International Labor Office, pp 129–156.

Anker, Richard, and Catherine Hein, eds. 1986. *Sex Inequalities in Urban Employment in the Third World*. London: MacMillan Press.

Anker, Richard, Mayra Buvinic, and Nadia H. Youssef. 1982. "Introduction." *Women's Roles and Population Trends in the Third World*. Eds. Richard Anker, Mayra Buvinic, and Nadia H. Youssef. London: Croom Helm, pp. 11–28.

Armanios, Febe. 2004. "Islam, Sunnis and Shiites." CRS Report for Congress. Congressional Research Service, The Library of Congress.

Assaad, R., and F. El-Hamidi. 2002. "Female Labor Supply in Egypt: Participation and Hours of Work." *Population Challenges in the Middle East and North Africa: Towards the 21st Century*. Ed. I. Sirageldin. ERF, Cairo.

Badawi, Leila. 1994. "Islam." *Women in Religion*. Eds. Jean Holm and John Bowker. London: Pinter, pp. 84–112.

Bahramitash, Roksanah. 2005. *Liberation from Liberalization, Gender and Globalization in South East Asia*. London: Zed Books.

———. 2007. "Iranian Women during the Reform Era (1994–2004), A Focus on Employment." *Journal of Middle East Women's Studies*, 3:2 (Spring), 86–109.

Bahramitash, Roksana and Hadi Salehi Esfahani. 2009. "Nimble Fingers No Longer! Women's Employment in Iran." *Contemporary*

Iran: Economy, Society, Politics. Ed. Ali Gheissari. New York: Oxford University Press.

Bank, Barbara J., and Peter M. Hall, eds. 1997. *Gender, Equity, and Schooling: Policy and Practice.* New York: Garland Publishing.

Barlas, Asma. 2002. *"Believing Women" in Islam: Unreading Patriarchal Interpretations of the Qur'an.* Austin: University of Texas Press.

Barrett, David, B. 1982. *World Christian Encyclopedia: A Comparative Study of Churches and Religions in the Modern World, AD 1900–2000.* New York: Oxford University Press.

Basu, Alaka, M. 1997. "The Politicization of Fertility to Achieve non-Demographic Objectives." *Population Studies,* 51, 5–18.

———. 2000. "Conditioning Factors for Fertility Decline in Bengal: History, Language, Identity, and Openness to Innovation." *Population and Development Review,* 26:4, 761–793.

Becker, Gary. 1991. *Treatise on the Family.* Cambridge, MA: Harvard University Press.

Beinin, Joel, and Joe Stork, eds. 1996. *Political Islam, Essays from Middle East Report.* Berkeley, CA: University of California Press.

Bell, Daniel. 1973. *The Coming of Post-Industrial Society.* New York: Basic Books.

———. 1976. *The Cultural Contradictions of Capitalism.* New York: Basic Books.

———. 1999. *The Coming of Post-Industrial Society: A Venture in Social Forecasting.* New York: Basic Books.

Beneria, Lourdes, and Gita Sen. 1982. "Class and Gender Inequalities and Women's Role in Economic Development: Theoretical and Practical Implications." *Feminist Studies,* 8:1 (Spring), 157–176.

———. 1986. "Accumulation, Reproduction, and Women's Role in Economic Development: Boserup Revisited." *Women's Work, Development and the Division of Labor by Gender.* Eds. E. Leacock and H. Safa. Massachusetts: Bergin and Garvey Publishers, pp. 141–157.

Beneria, Lourdes, and Shelly Feldman, eds. 1992. *Unequal Burden: Economic Crises, Persistent Poverty, and Women's Work.* Boulder: Westview Press.

Berger, Peter L. 1963. *Invitation to Sociology: A Humanistic Perspective.* New York: Knopf Doubleday Publishing Group.

Berik Gunseli, and Nilufer Cagatay. 1992. "Industrialization Strategies and Gender Composition of Manufacturing Employment in Turkey." *Issues in Contemporary Economics, Women's Work in the World Economy.* Vol. 4. Eds. Nancy Folbre et al. Hong Kong: Macmillan.

Bianchi, Suzanne, Lynne Casper, and Pia Peltola. 1999. "A Cross-National Look at Married Women's Earnings Dependency." *Gender Issues*, 17:3 (Summer), 3–33.

Bills, David B. 2004. *The Sociology of Education and Work*. Malden, MA: Blackwell Publishing.

Birdsall, Nancy, and William McGreevey. 1983. "Women, poverty, and development." in *Women and Poverty in the Third World*. Eds. Myra Buvinic, Margaret A. Lycette, and William McGreevy. Baltimore: The Johns Hopkins University Press, pp. 3–13.

Birks, J.S., I.J. Seccombe, and C.A. Sinclair. 1988. "Labour Migration in the Arab Gulf States: Patterns, Trends and Prospects." *International Migration*, 26:3 (September), 267–286. http://www.ncbi.nlm.nih.gov/entrez/query.fcgi?cmd=Retrieve&db=PubMed&list_uids=12342068&dopt=Abstract.

Black, C.E. 1966. *The Dynamics of Modernization*. New York: Harper and Row.

Black, N., and A. Cottrell. 1981. *Women and World Change*. Beverly Hills, CA: Sage.

Bloom, David E., and Richard Freeman. 1986. "The Effects of Rapid Population Growth on Labor Supply and Employment in Developing Countries." *Population and Development Review*, 12: 3, 381–414.

Bolles, L. 1983. "Kitchen Hit by Priorities: Employed Working-Class Jamaican Women Confront the IMF." *Women, Men and the International Division of Labor*. Eds. J. Nash and M.P. Fernandez-Kelly. Albany: State University of New York Press, pp. 138–159.

Bongaarts, John. 1978. "A Framework for Analyzing the Proximate Determinants of Fertility." *Population and Development Review*, 4:1, 105–132.

Bose, Ashis. 2005. "Beyond Hindu Muslim Growth Rates: Understanding Socioeconomic Reality." *Economic and Political Weekly* (January 29), 370–374.

Boserup, Ester. 1970. *Women's Role in Economic Development*. London: Allen and Unwin.

———. 1986. "Shifts in the Determinants of Fertility in the Developing World." *Forward From Malthus: The State of Population Theory*. Eds. D. Coleman and R. Schofield. New York: Oxford University Press, pp. 239–294.

———. 1990. "Economic Change and the Roles of Women." *Persistent Inequalities: Women and World Development*. Ed. Irene Tinker. New York: Oxford University Press, pp. 123–149.

———. 1990. "Population, the Status of Women, and Rural Development." And "Inequality Between the Sexes." *Economic and Demographic Relations in Development*. Ed. Ester Boserup. Baltimore: Johns Hopkins University Press, pp. 14–24.

Bossen, Laurel H. 1984. *The Redivision of Labor: Women and Economic Choice in Four Guatemalan Communities*. Albany: SUNY Series in the Anthropology of Work.

Bowen, Wayne H. 2008. *The History of Saudi Arabia*. Westport, Connecticut: Greenwood Press.

Brand, Laurie. 1998. *Women, the State, and the Political Liberalization: Middle Eastern and North African Experiences*. New York: Columbia University Press.

Brewster, Karin, and Roland Rindfuss. 2000. "Fertility and Women's Employment in Industrialized Nations." *Annual Review of Sociology*, 26, 271–296.

Briegel, Toni, and Jaye Zivkovic. 2008. "Financial Empowerment of Women in the United Arab Emirates." *Journal of Middle East Women's Studies*, 4:2 (Spring), 87–99.

Britton, Mary, Yean-Ju Lee, and William Parish. 1995. "Married Women's Employment in Rapidly Industrializing Societies." *American Journal of Sociology*, 100:5 (March), 1099–1130.

Bruce, Judith, and Daisy Dwyer. 1988. "Introduction." *A Home Divided: Women and Income in the Third World*. Eds. Daisy Dwyer and Judith Bruce. Stanford: Stanford University Press, pp.1–19.

Cain, Mead. 1986. "The Consequence of Reproduction Failure: Dependence, Mobility and Mortality Among the Elderly of Rural South Asia." *Population Studies*, 40, 375–388.

Cain, Mead, Syeda Rokeya Khanom, and Shamsun Nashar. 1979. "Class, Patriarchy, and Women's Work in Bangladesh." *Population and Development Review*, 5 (September), 405–438.

Caldwell, John. 1976. "Toward a Restatement of Demographic Transition Theory." *Population and Development Review* 2:3–4, pp. 321–366.

Caldwell, John C. 1982. *Theory of Fertility Decline*. London and New York: Academic Press.

Cardeso, Fernando H., and Enzo Faletto. 1979. *Dependency and Development in Latin America*. Berkeley: University of California Press.

Castles, Stephen, and M.J. Miller. 1993. *The Age of Migration: International Population Movements in the Modern World*. New York: Guilford Press.

Castro Martin, Teresa. 1995. "Women's Education and Fertility: Results from 26 Demographic and Health Surveys." *Studies in Family Planning*, 26:4 (July–August), 187–202.

Castro Martin, Teresa, and Fatima Juarez. 1995. "The Impact of Women's Education on Fertility in Latin American: Searching for Explanations." *International Family Planning Perspectives*, 21:2, 52–57.

Chamie, Mary. 1985. *Women of the World: Near East and North Africa*. Washington, D.C.: U.S. Department of Commerce, Bureau of the Census, and U.S. Agency for International Development, Office of Women in Development.

Charrad, Mounira M. 2001. *States and Women's Rights: The Making of Postcolonial Tunisia, Algeria, and Morocco*. Berkeley: University of California Press.

Cho, Uhn, and Hagen Koo. 1983. "Economic Development and Women's Work in a Newly Industrializing Country: The Case of Korea." *Development and Change*, 14, 515–532.

CIA World Facts Book. (1992, 2000, 2003). http://www.cia.gov/cia/publications/factbook/index.html.

Clark, Roger, Thomas W. Ramsbey, and Emily Steir Adler. 1991. "Culture, Gender, and Labor Force Participation: A Cross-National Study." *Gender and Society*, 5:1 (March), 47–66.

Coale, Ansley J. 1974. "The History of the Human Population." *Scientific American*, 231 (September), 41–51.

Collins, Randall. 1979. *The Credential Society: An Historical Sociology of Education and Stratification*. New York: Academic Press.

Collver, Andrew, and Eleanor Langlois. 1962. "The Female Labor Force in Metropolitan Areas: An International Comparison." *Economic Development and Cultural Change*, 10, 367–385.

Corden, W.M., and P.J. Neary. 1982. "Booming Sector and Deindustrialization in a Small Open Economy." *The Economic Journal*, 92 (December), 825–848.

Cotter, David, Joan Hermsen, and Reeve Vanneman. 2004. *Gender Inequality at Work*. Washington DC: Population Reference Bureau. http://www.prb.org/Articles/2004/GenderInequalityatWork.aspx. Retrieved on August 30, 2007.

Dasgupta, Partha S. 1995. Population, Poverty and the Local Environment. *Scientific American*, 272:2, 4045.

Davis, K. and J. Blake. 1956. "Social Structure and Fertility: An Analytic Framework." *Economic Development and Cultural Change*, 4, 211–235.

De Soya, Indra, and John O'Neal. 1999. "Boom or Bane? Reassessing the Productivity of Foreign Direct Investment with New Data." *American Sociological Review*, 64, 766–782.

Debeir, Jean-Claude, Jean-Claude Deleage, and Daniel Hemery. 1991. *In the Servitude of Power, Energy and Civilisation through the Ages.* London: Zed Books.

Deere, C., and M. Leon de Leal. 1981. "Peasant Production, Proletarianization, and the Sexual Division of Labor in the Andes." *Signs: Journal of Women in Culture and Society,* 7, 338–360.

DiMaggio, Paul. 1994. "Culture and Economy." *The Handbook of Economic Sociology.* Eds. Neil Smalser and Richard Swedberg. New York and Princeton: Russell Sage Foundation and Princeton University Press, pp. 27–57.

Dixon, Ruth B. 1982. "Women in Agriculture: Counting the Labor Force in Developing Countries." *Population and Development Review,* 8:3, 539–566.

Docquier, F., and A. Marfouk. 2005. "International migration by educational attainment, 1999–2000." *International Migration, Remittances and the Brain Drain.* Eds. M. Schiff and C. Ozden. World Bank Report on Brain Drain 2005.

Dollar, David. 1992. "Outward-Oriented Developing Economies Really Do Grow More Rapidly: Evidence from 95 LDCs, 1976–1985." *Economic Development and Cultural Change,* 13:79, 523–544.

Donahoe, Debra Anne. 1999. "Measuring Women's Work in Developing Countries." *Population and Development Review,* 25:3 (September 1999), 543–576.

Donaldson, P.J., and A. Tsui. 1990. "The International Family Planning Movement." *Population Bulletin,* 45:3 (November), 1–45.

Dubeck, Paula, and Dana Dunn. 2002. *Workplace/Women's Place: An Anthology.* Los Angeles: Roxbury.

Durand, John D. 1975. *The Labor Force in Economic Development.* Princeton: Princeton University Press.

El-Wasat. 2003. As cited in UNIFEM, Progress of Arab Women.

Encyclopedia of Islam and the Muslim World. 2004. Macmillan Reference.

Enders, K. 2001. *Yemen in the 1990s.* International Monetary Fund, November.

Energy Statistics Yearbook. 1999. United Nations—Department of Economics and Social Affair, New York.

Enloe, C. 1983. "Women Textile Workers in the Militarization of Southeast Asia." *Women, Men and the International Division of Labor.* Eds. J. Nash and M.P. Fernandez-Kelly. Albany: State University of New York Press, 407–425.

Esping-Andersen, Gosta. 1990. *The Three Worlds of Welfare Capitalism*. New Jersey. Princeton University Press.

Evans, M.D.R., and Helcio U. Saraiva. 1993. "Women's Labour Force Participation and Socioeconomic Development: Influences of Local Context and Individual Characteristics in Brazil." *The British Journal of Sociology*, 44:1 (March 1993), 25–51.

Evans, Peter. 1995. *Embedded Autonomy: States and the Industrial Transformation*. Princeton, NJ: Princeton University Press.

Evans, Peter, and Michael Timberlake. 1980. "Dependence, Inequality, and the Growth of the Tertiary." *American Sociological Review*, 45, 531–552.

Fagley, R. 1965. "Doctrines and Attitudes of major Religions with Regard to Fertility," Paper presented at the U.N. World Population Conference, Belgrade, quoted in O. Schieffelin, ed. 1967. *Muslim Attitudes Toward Family Planning*. New York: The Population Council.

Fargues, Philippe. 2003. "Women in Arab Countries: Challenging the Patriarchal System?" *Population et Societes*, 387 (February).

Foucault, Michel. 1966. *Les Mots et les choses. Une archéologie des sciences humaines*. Trans. Alan Sheridan as *The Order of Things: An Archaeology of the Human Sciences*. New York: Vintage, 1970.

———. 1969. *L'Archéologie du savoir*. Trans. Alan Sheridan as *The Archaeology of Knowledge*. New York: Pantheon, 1972.

Fernandez-Kelly, M.P. 1983. "Mexican Border Industrialization, Female Labor Force Participation, and Migration." *Women, Men and International Division of Labor*. Eds. J. Nash and M.P. Fernandez-Kelly. Albany: State University of New York Press, pp. 205–223.

Fernandez-Kelly, Patricia, and Jon Shefner, eds. 2006. *Out of the Shadows: Political Action and the Informal Economy in Latin America*. University Park, PA: The Pennsylvania State University Press.

Firebaugh, Glenn. 1996. "Does Foreign Capital Harm Poor Nations? New Estimates based on Dixon and Boswell's Measures of Capital Penetration." *American Journal of Sociology*, 102, 563–575.

———. 1999. "Empirics of World Income Inequality." *American Journal of Sociology*, 104, 1597–1630.

Fong, M. 1975. "Female Labor Force Participation in a Modernizing Society: Malaysia and Singapore, 1921–1957." Papers of the East-West Population Institute No. 34. Honolulu: East-West Center.

Frank, Andre Gunder. 1966. "The Development of Underdevelopment." *Monthly Review*, 18:4, 17–31.

Freedman, Robert. 1995. "Asia's Recent Fertility Decline and Prospects for Future Demographic Change." *Asia-Pacific Population Research Reports*, no. 1 (January 1995), 1–28.

Fuentes, Annette, and Barbara Ehrenreich. 1983. *Women in the Global Factory*. New York: Institute for New Communications, South End Press.

Giddens, Anthony, Mitchell Duneier, and Richard Appelbaum. 2005. *Introduction to Sociology*. W.W. Norton and Company.

Gonzalez, Salazar G. 1976. "Participation of Women in the Mexican Labor Force." *Sex and Class in Latin America*. Eds. J. Nash and H.I. Safa. New York: Praeger, pp. 182–201. Gould, W.T.S. 1993. *People and Education in the Third World*. London: Longman.

Graff, J. Harvey. "Literacy, Education, and Fertility, Past and Present: A Critical Review." *Population and Development Review*, 5:1 (March 1979), 105–140.

Greenhalgh, Susan. 1985. "Sexual Stratification: The Other Side of 'Growth with Equity' in East Asia." *Population and Development Review*, 11, 265–314.

Haddad Yazbeck, Yvonne, and John L. Esposito, eds. 1998. *Islam, Gender, and Social Change*. New York: Oxford University Press.

———. 2001. *Daughters of Abraham: Feminist Thought in Judaism, Christianity, and Islam*. Gainesville, FL: University of Florida Press.

Haghighat, Elhum. 2002. "Culture, Development and Female Labor Force Participation: Disaggregating Different Sectors." *International Review of Sociology*, 12:3, 343–362.

———. 2003. "Quest for Solidarity, Resisting Patriarchy, and Seeking Connection: An Analysis of Persian Poetry Written by Women." *Identities: Journal of Politics, Gender and Culture*, 2:1, 97–120.

———. 2005. "Neopatriarchal State, Islam and Female Labour Force Participation: A Reconsideration." *International Journal of Sociology and Social Policy*, 25:10, 84–105.

———. 2005. "A Comparative Analysis of Neopatriarchy and Female Labor Force Participation in Islamic Countries." *Electronic Journal of Sociology*, 1:1, 1–26.

Haghighat-Sordellini, Ehlum. 2009. "Determinants of Female Labor Force Participation: A Focus on Muslim Countries. *International Review of Sociology—Revue Internationale de Sociologie*, 19:1, 103–125.

Haifa, R. Al-Leil. 1996. "Muslim Women between Tradition and Modernity: The Islamic Perspective." *Journal of Muslim Minority Affairs*, 16:1 (January), 99, 12 P.

Hakim, Catherine. 1993. "Segregated and Integrated Occupations: A New Approach to Analysing Social Change." *European Sociological Review*, 9, 289–314.

———. 1997. "A Sociological Perspective on Part-time Work." *Between Equalization and Marginalization: Women Working Part-Time in Europe and the United States of America*. Eds. H.P. Blossfeld and C. Hakim. Oxford: Oxford University Press, pp. 22–70.

———. 2004. *Key Issues in Women's Work, Female Diversity and the Polarisation of Women's Employment* (2nd ed.) London: Glasshouse Press.

Hanjal, J. 1965. "European Marriage Patterns in Perspective." *Population in History: Essays in Historical Demography*. Eds. D.V. Glass and D.E.C. Eversley. London: Edward Arnold, pp. 101–143.

Hatem, Mervat. 1998. "Secularist and Islamist Discourses on Modernity in Egypt and Evolution of the Postcolonial Nation-State." *Islam, Gender, and Social Change*. Eds. Yvonne Haddad and John L. Esposito. New York: Oxford University Press, pp. 88–99.

Heckman, James. 1980. *Female Labor Supply: Theory and Estimation*. Princeton, NJ: Princeton University Press.

Hein, Simon. 1992. "Trade Strategy and the Dependency Hypothesis: A Comparison of Policy, Foreign Investment and Economic Growth in Latin America and East Asia." *Economic Development and Cultural Change*, 13:79, 495–521.

Heynerman, Stephen P. 1997. "The Quality of Education in the Middle East and North Africa." *International Journal of Educational Development*, 17:4, 449–466.

Hijab, Nadia. 1988 and 1994. *Womanpower: The Arab debate on women at work*. Cambridge University Press.

Hoodfar, Homa. 1996. "Survival strategies and the political economy of low-income households in Cairo." *Development, Change and Gender in Cairo*. Eds. Dianne Singerman and Homa Hoodfar. Bloomington: Indiana University Press, pp. 1–26.

———. 1996. "Circumventing Legal Limitation: Mahr and Marriage Negotiation in Egyptian Low Income Communities." *Shifting Boundaries in Marriage and Divorce in Muslim Communities*. Ed. Homa Hoodfar. Montpelier, France: Women Living Under Muslim Laws, pp. 121–142.

Hoodfar, Homa, and Samad Assadpour. 2000. "The Politics of Population Policy in the Islamic Republic of Iran." *Studies in Family Planning*, 31:1 (March), 19–34.

Hourani, Albert. 2002. *A History of the Arab Peoples*. England: Clays Ltd.

Hu-DeHart, Evelyn. 2003. "Globalization and its Discontents: Exposing the Underside." *Frontiers*, 24:2&3, 244–260.

Hughes, Michael, Carolyn Kroehler, and James Vander Zanden. 1999. *Sociology, the Core* (5th ed.). Boston: McGraw Hill.

Human Rights Watch. Middle East/North Africa. "Bad Dreams, Exploitation and Abuse of Migrant Workers in Saudi Arabia." http://hrw.org/mideast/saudi/labor/. Retrieved on August 9, 2007.

Human Rights Watch. Middle East/North Africa. "Migrant Communities in Saudi Arabia." http://hrw.org/reports/2004/saudi0704/4.htm. Retrieved on August 9, 2007.

Humana, Charles. 1986. *World Human Rights Guide*. New York: Facts on File Publications.

———. 1992. *World Human Rights Guide* (3rd ed.). New York: Oxford University Press.

Huntington, Samuel. 1968. *Political Order in Changing Societies*. Conn.: Yale University Press.

———. 1996. *The Clash of Civilizations and the Remaking of World Order*. New York: Simon & Schuster.

Iglitzen, L., and R. Ross, eds. 1986. *Women in the World: 1975–1985, The Women's Decade*. Santa Barbara, CA: ABC-CLIO.

Inglehart, Ronald, and Wayne Baker. 2000. "Modernization, Cultural Change, and the Persistence of Traditional Values." *American Sociological Review*, 65 (February), 19–51.

Inkles, A., and D.H. Smith. 1974. *Becoming Modern: Individual Change in Six Developing Countries*. Cambridge, MA: Harvard University Press.

The Institute of Islamic Information and Education, http://www.iiie.net/intl/popstats.html.

International Labor Office, Global Employment Trends for Women. 2007. Table 3.

International Labor Office. 1986. *Economically Active Population—Estimates, 1950–1980, Projections, 1985–2025*. Six volumes. Geneva: International Labor Office.

International Labor Office. http://laborsta.ilo.org.

Iyer, Sriya. 2002. *Demography and Religion in India*. New Delhi: Oxford University Press.

Jacobson, Joyce. 1994. "Sex Segregation at Work: Trends and Predictions. *Social Science Journal*, 31:2, 153–168.

Jain, Devaki. 1990. "Development Theory and Practice: Insights Emerging from Women's Experience." *Economic and Political Weekly*, 7 (July), 1454–1455.

Jeffery, Roger, and P. Jeffery. 1997. *Population, Gender and Politics*. Cambridge, England: Cambridge University Press.

Jeffery, Roger, and P. Jeffery. 2002. "A Population out of Control? Myths about Muslim Fertility in Contemporary India." *World Development*, 30:10, 1805–1822.

Jelin, E. 1977. "Migration and the Labor Force Participation of Latin American Women: The Domestic Servants in the Cities." *Signs*, 3, 129–141.

Joakes, Susan P. 1987. *Women in the World Economy: An INSTRAW Study.* New York: Oxford University Press.

Johnson, Allan G. 1997. *The Gender Knot: Unraveling Our Patriarchal Legacy.* Temple University Press.

Jones, Gavin. 1984. "Economic Growth and Changing Female Employment Structures in the Cities of Southeast and East Asia." *Women in the Urban and Industrial Workforce: Southeast and East Asia.* Eds. Gavin W. Jones. Honolulu: University of Hawaii Press, pp. 17–60.

Joseph, Suad, and Afsaneh Najmabadi. 2005. *Encyclopedia of Women and Islamic Cultures: Family Law and Politics.* Brill Academic Publishers.

Kabeer, Neila. 1999. "Resources, Agency, Achievements: Reflections on the Measurement of Women's Empowerment." *Development and Change*, 30 (1999), 435–464.

Kabeer, Naila, and Simeen Mahmud. 2004. "Globalization, Gender, and Poverty: Bangladeshi Women Workers in Export and Local Markets." *Journal of International Development*, 16 (January), 93–109.

Kamrava, Mehran. 1990. *Revolution in Iran: Roots of Turmoil.* London: Routledge.

———. 1992. *Revolutionary Politics.* New York: Praeger.

———. 1998. *Democracy in the Balance: Culture & Society in the Middle East.* New York: Chatham House.

———. 1999. *Cultural Politics in the Third World.* London: University College of London Press.

———. 2005. *The Modern Middle East: A Political History since World War I.* Berkeley, CA: University of California Press.

———, ed. 2006. *The New Voices of Islam: Rethinking Politics and Modernity.* Berkeley, CA: University of California Press & London: I. B. Tauris.

———, ed. 2007. *The New Voices of Islam: Rethinking Politics and Modernity—A Reader.* Berkeley, CA: University of California Press.

———. 2008. *Iran's Intellectual Revolution.* Cambridge.

———. 2008 [1996]. *Understanding Comparative Politics: A Framework for Analysis.* 2nd ed. London: Routledge.

Kandiyoti, Deniz. 1988. "Bargaining with Patriarchy." *Gender and Society*, 2:3 (September), 274–290.

———. 1992. "Islam and Patriarchy: A comparative Perspective." *Women in Middle Eastern History: Shifting Boundaries in Sex and Gender*. Eds. Nikki Keddie and Beth Baron. New Haven, Connecticut: Yale University Press, pp. 23–42.

———. 2001. "The Politics of Gender and the Conundrums of Citizenship." *Women and Power in the Middle East*. Eds. Suad Joseph and Susan Slyomovics. Philadelphia: University of Pennsylvania Press, pp. 52–58.

———, ed. 1996. *Gendering the Middle East: Emerging Perspectives*. Syracuse University Press.

Kentor, Jeffrey. 1981. "Structural Determinants of Peripheral Urbanization: The Effects of International Dependence." *American Sociological Review*, 46, 201–211.

Kenworthy, L., and M. Malami. 1999. "Gender Inequality in Political Representation: A Worldwide Comparative Analysis." *Social Forces*, 78:1 (September), 235–268.

Khoury, Nabil F., and Valentine M. Moghadam. 1995. *Gender and Development in the Arab World, Women's Economic Participation: Patterns and Policies*. London: Zed Books.

King, Mary. 2001. "Familial Economics or Patriarchal Economic Regimes? MENA in Comparative Perspective." Paper presented at the Second Mediterranean Social and Political Research Meeting, Florence, Italy, March 21–25.

King, Stephen J. 1998. "Beyond Colonialism and Nationalism in North Africa." *Arab Studies Quarterly* (ASQ) (March 22).

Kirk, Dudley. 1971. "A New Demographic Transition?" *Rapid Population Growth*. Ed. National Academy of Sciences. Baltimore: Johns Hopkins Press, pp. 123–147.

Koury, Philip S., and Joseph Kostiner, ed. 1991. *Tribes and State Formation in the Middle East*. Berkeley: University of California Press.

Larsen, Janet. 2001. "Iran's Birth Rate Plummeting at Record Pace: Success Provides a Model for other Developing Countries." Earth Policy Institute. http://www.earth-policy.org/Updates/Update4ss.htm. Retrieved on August 30, 2007.

Lattouf, Mirna. 2004. *Women, Education, and Socialization in Modern Lebanon*. New York: University Press of America.

Laupham, R.J., and Parker Mauldin. 1985. "Contraceptive Prevalence: The Influence of Organized Family Planning Programs." *Studies in Family Planning*, 16:3, 117–137.

Lazerg, Marnia. 2009. *Questioning the Veil, Open Letters to Muslim Women*. Princeton, NJ: Princeton University Press.

Lerner, Gerda. 1986. *The Creation of Patriarchy*. New York: Oxford University Press.

Levy, Marion J. 1966. *Modernization and the Structure of Societies: A Setting for International Affairs*. Princeton: Princeton University Press.

Lewin-Epstein, Noah, and Moshe Semyonov. 1992. "Modernization and Subordination: Arab. Women in the Israeli Labor Force." *European Sociological Review*, 8:1, 39–51.

Lewis, Bernard. 1992. *Race and Slavery in the Middle East*. New York: Oxford University Press.

Lim, Lin Lean. "Female Labour-force Participation, Trends in Female Labour Force Participation and Fertility." Gender Promotion Programme (GENPROM), International Labour Office, Geneva, Switzerland, United Nations: http://www.un.org/esa/population/publications/completingfertility/RevisedLIMpaper.PDF. Retrieved on August 30, 2007.

Lockhat, Haseena. 2004. *Female Genital Mutilation: Treating the Tears*. London: Middlesex University Press.

Lopez-Claros, Augusto, and Saadia Zahidi. 2005. *Women's Empowerment: Measuring the Global Gender Gap*. Switzerland: World Economic Forum.

Luo, Guifen. 2005. "Effects of Rural-Urban Migration on Rural Female Workers, A Case Study of Chinese Rural Women." Paper for NACS Conferences, Helsinki, June 7–9, 2005.

Mabro, Robert. 1988. "Industrialization." *The Middle East*. Ed. Michael Adams. New York: Facts on File, pp. 687–696.

Macaud, C.A., ed. 1964. *Tunisia: The Politics of Modernization*. New York: Praeger.

Makhlouf Obermeyer, *See Obermeyer*.

Malhotra, A. 1997. "Gender and the Timing of Marriage: Rural-Urban Differences in Java." *Journal of Marriage and the Family*, 59:2, 434–450.

Malhotra, Anju, Reeve Vanneman, and Sunita Kishor. 1995. "Fertility, Dimensions of Patriarchy, and Development in India." *Population and Development Review*, 21 (June), 281–305.

Mammen, Kristin, and Christina Paxton. 2000. "Women's Work and Economic Development." *Journal of Economic Perspectives*, 14 (Autumn), 141–64.

Marion, J. Levy, Jr., *Modernization and the Structure of Societies*. Princeton, NJ: Princeton University Press, pp. 35–36.

Marshal, Susan. 1985. "Development, Dependence, and Gender Inequality in the Third World." *International Studies Quarterly*, 29, 217–240.

Martin, Philip, and Jonas Widgren. 1996. *International Migration: A Global Challenge.* Population Bulletin, Vol. 51, No. 1, April. Washington D.C.: Population Reference Bureau.

Marx, Karl. 1973. *Foundations of the Critique of Political Economy.* New York: Vintage Books.

Mason, Karen Oppenheim. 1986. "The Status of Women: Conceptual and Methodological Issues in Demographic Studies." *Social Forces*, 1:2, 284–300.

———. 2001. "Gender and Family Systems in the Fertility Transition." *Global Fertility Transition.* Eds. Rodolfo A. Bulatao and John B. Casterline. New York: Population Council, pp. 160–176.

Mauldin, Parker, and Robert J. Lapham. 1984. "Family Planning Program Effort and Birthrate Decline in Developing Countries." *International Family Planning Perspectives*, 10:4, 109–118.

———. 1985. "Contraceptive Prevalence: The Influence of Organized Family Planning Programs." *Studies in Family Planning*, 16:3, 117–137.

McKeown, Thomas. 1976. *The Modern Rise of Population.* New York: Academic Press.

Mensch, Barbara, Susheela Singh, and John Casterline. 2005. "Trends in the Timing of First Marriage among Men and Women in the Developing World." *The Population Council*, no. 202.

Mernissi, Fatima. 1991. *The Veil and the Male Elite: A Feminist Interpretation of Women's Rights in Islam.* Readings, MA: Addison-Wesley.

Metz, Helen Chapin, ed. 1987. *Libya: A Country Study.* Washington: GPO for the Library of Congress, 1987.

Micaud, C.A., ed. 1964. *Tunisia: The Politics of Modernization.* New York: Praeger.

Middle East and North Africa. (1995) (41st ed.). London: Europa Publications Limited.

Mir-Hosseini, Ziba. 1993, 2000. *Marriage on Trial: Islamic Family Law in Iran and Morocco.* London: I. B. Tauris.

———. 1999. *Islam and Gender.* Princeton, NJ: Princeton University Press.

Moghadam, Valentine. 1988. "Women, Work and Ideology in the Islamic Republic." *International Journal of Middle East Studies*, 20, 221–243.

Moghadam, Valentine. 1992a. "Patriarchy and the Politics of Gender in Modernizing Societies: Iran, Pakistan and Afghanistan." *International Sociology*, 7 (March), 35–53.

———. 1992b. "Development and Patriarchy: The Middle East and North Africa in Economic and Demographic Transition." *World Institute for Development Economics Research of the United Nations University (WIDER)*. WP 99, July.

———. 1999. "Gender and Globalization: Female Labor Force and Women's Mobilization." *Journal of World Systems Research*, V(2): 367–388.

———. 2004 and 1993. *Modernizing Women: Gender and Social Change in the Middle East*. Boulder and London: Lynne Reinner Publishers.

Moghadam, Valentine. 1988. 2004. "Patriarchy in Transition: Women and the Changing Family in the Middle East." *Journal of Comparative Family Studies*, 35:2 (Spring), 137–162.

Moghadam, Valentine, ed. 1994. *Gender and National Identity: Women and Politics in Muslim Society*. London: Zed Books. United Nations University World Institute for Development Economics Research (UNU/WIDER).

Moore, Laura, and Reeve Vanneman. 2003. "Context Matters: Effects of the Proportion of Fundamentalists on Gender Attitudes." *Social Forces*, 82:1, 115–139.

Moore, Wilbert E. 1979. *World Modernization: The Limits of Convergence*. New York: Elsevier.

Morgan, Phillip. S., Sharon Stash, Herbert Smith, and Karen Oppenheim Mason. 2002. "Muslim and non-Muslim Differentials in Female Autonomy and Fertility: Evidence from Four Asian Countries." *Population and Development Review*, 28:3, 517–537.

Musallam, Basim. 1983a. *Sex and Society in Islam, Birth Control Before the Nineteenth Century*. Cambridge, U.K.: Cambridge University Press.

———. 1983b. "Contraception and the Rights of Women." In *Sex and Society in Islam*, pp. 29–38.

Nabli, Mustapha. Conference on Higher Education in the Middle East and North Africa: Challenges and Opportunities for the 21st Century. Institute de Monde Arabe. May 23, 2002, World Bank Group, Middle East and North Africa. Retrieved on July 27, 2006: http://lnweb18.worldbank.org/mna/mena.nsf/Attachments/Education-Nabli/$File/HigherEducation-Nabli.pdf.

Nam, S. 1991. "Determinants of Female Labor Force Participation: A Study of Seoul, South Korea, 1970–1980." *Sociological Forum*, 6:4, 641–659.

Nash, J., and H.I. Safa. 1976. *Sex and Class in Latin America*. New York: Praeger.

Nash, June, and Maria Patricia Fernandez-Kelly, eds. 1983. *Women, Men and the International Division of Labor*. Albany, NY: SUNY Press.

Nashat, Guity, ed. 1983. *Women and Revolution in Iran*. Boulder, Colorado: Westview Press.

Nashat, Guity, and Judith E. Tucker. 1998. *Women in the Middle East and North Africa*. Bloomington: Indiana University Press.

Nasr, Seyyed Hossein. 2000. *Ideas and Realities of Islam*. Chicago: ABC International Group.

National Standards Association. 1987. *Worldwide Government Directory of 1987–1988*. Bethesda, Maryland.

Newland, Kathleen. 1979. *International Migration, The Search for Work*. Washington D.C.: World Watch Institute.

Newman, K. 1981. "Women and Law: Land Tenure in Africa." *Women and World Change*. Eds. N. Black and A.B. Cottrell. Beverly Hills, CA: Sage, pp. 120–138.

Nielsen, Joyce McCarl. 1990. *Sex and Gender in Society: Perspectives on Stratification* (2nd ed.). Illinois: Waveland Press.

Notestein, Frank W., Dudley Kirk, and Sheldon Segal. 1969. "The Problem of Population Control." *Population Dilemma* (2nd ed.). Ed. Philip M. Hauser. Englewood Cliffs, NJ: Prentice Hall, pp. 130–167.

Nuss, S. (1989). *Women in the World of Work, Statistical Analysis and Projections to the Year 2000*. Geneva: International Labor Office.

Nuss, Shirley, Ettore Denti, and David Viry. 1989. *Women in the World of Work: Statistical Analysis and Projections to the Year 2000*. Geneva: International Labour Office.

Oakley, Ann. 1974. *Women's Work*. New York, NY: Vintage Books.

Obermeyer, Carla Makhlouf. 1992. "Islam, Women, and Politics: The Demography of Arab Countries." *Population and Development Review*, 18:1 (March), 33–60.

———. 1994. "Reproductive Choice in Islam: Gender and State in Iran and Tunisia." *Studies in Family Planning*, 25:1, 41–51.

———. 1997. "Son Preference and Differential Treatment in Morocco and Tunisia." *Studies in Family Planning*, 28:3 (September), 235–244.

O'Kelly, C., and L. Carney. 1985. *Women and Men in Society*. Belmont, CA: Wadsworth.

Olmsted, Jennifer. 2003. "Reexamining the Fertility Puzzle in the Middle East and North Africa." *Women and Globalization in the*

Arab Middle East: Gender, Economy and Society. Eds. Eleanor Doumato and Marsha Pripstein-Posusney. Boulder: Lynne Reinner, pp. 73–92.

———. 2005. "Is Paid Work the (Only) Answer? Neo-liberalism, Arab Women's Well-being, and the Social Contract." *Journal of Middle East Women's Studies*, 1:2 (Spring), 112–139.

Omran, Abdel Rahim. 1992. *Family Planning in the Legacy of Islam.* New York: Routledge.

Ong, A. 1983. "Global Industries and Malay Peasants in Peninsular Malaysia." *Women, Men and the International Division of Labor.* Eds. J. Nash and M.P. Fernandez-Kelly. Albany: State University of New York Press, pp. 426–441.

Oppenheimer, Valerie K. 1970. "The Female Labor Force in the United States: Demographic and Economic Factors Governing its Growth and Changing Composition." *Population Monograph Series*, no. 5. Berkeley: University of California Press.

Orloff, Ann S. 1993. "Gender and the Social Rights of Citizenship." *American Sociological Review*, 58:3, 303–328.

Pampel Fred C., and Kazuko Tanaka. 1986. "Economic Development and Female Labor Force Participation: A Reconsideration." *Social Forces*, 64:3 (March), 599–619.

Papanek, Hanna. 1973. "Purdah: Separate Worlds and Symbolic Shelter." *Comparative Studies in Society and History*, 15:3, 289–325.

———. 1990. "To Each Less than She Needs, from Each More than She Can Do: Allocations, Entitlements, and Value." *Persistent Inequalities: Women and World Development.* Ed. Irene Tinker. New York: Oxford University Press, pp. 162–181.

Parrenas, Rhacel Salazar. 2000. "Migrant Filipina Domestic Workers and the International Division of Reproductive Labor." *Gender and Society*, 14:4, 560–580.

———. 2001. "Transgressing the Nation-State: The Partial Citizenship and 'Imagined (Global) Community' of Migrant Filipina Domestic Workers." *Signs: Journal of Women in Culture & Society*, 2:4 (Summer), 1129, 26p.

Parson, T. 1971. *The System of Modern Societies.* Englewood Cliffs, NJ: Prentice-Hall.

Patai, R. 1967. *Women in the Modern World.* New York: Free Press.

Pateman, Carole. 1988. *Sexual Contract.* Standford, CA: Stanford University Press.

Philip Morgan, S. Sharon Stash, Herbert L. Smith, and Karen Oppenheim Mason. 2002. "Muslim and Non-Muslim Differences in Female Autonomy and Fertility: Evidence from Four Asian Countries." *Population and Development Review*, 28:3, 515–537.

Pillarisetti, J. Ram, and Mark McGillivray. 1998. "Human Development and Gender Empowerment: Methodological and Measurement Issues." *Development Policy Review*, 16 (1998), 197–203.

Pollack, Kenneth M. 2004. *The Persian Puzzle: The Conflict Between Iran and America*. New York: Random House.

Population of Muslims around the World. (2002). http://www.Islamicweb.com.

Portes, A., and J. Walton. 1981. *Labor, Class and the International System*. New York: Academic Press.

Pyle, Jean Larson. 1990. *The State and Women in the Economy*. Albany: State University of New York Press.

Ramirez, F. 1981. "Statism, Equality, and Housewifery: A Cross-national Analysis." *Pacific Sociological Review*, 24:2, 175–195.

Rashad, Hoda, and Magued Osman. 2003. "Nuptiality in Arab Countries: Changes and Implication." *The New Arab Family, Cairo Papers in Social Sciences*, vol. 24, nos. 1–2. Ed. Nicholas Hopkins. Cairo: The American University in Cairo Press, pp. 20–50.

Rawl, John. 1999 [1971]. *A Theory of Justice*. Oxford: Oxford University Press.

Rispler-Chaim, Vardit. 1999. "The Right Not to Be Born: Abortion of the Disadvantaged fetus in Contemporary Fatwas." *Muslim World*, 89:2, 130–143.

Roberts, Timmons J., and Amy Hite. 2000. *From Modernization to Globalization: Perspectives on Development and Social Change*. London: Wiley-Blackwell Publishers.

Ross, John A., Marjorie Rich, Janet P. Molzan, and Michael Pensak. 1988. *Family Planning and Child Survival: 100 Developing Countries*. Center for Population and Family Health, Columbia University Press.

Ross, Michael. 2008. "Oil, Islam, and Women." *American Political Science Review*, 102:1 (February), 107–123.

Rothenberg, Paula. 1988. *Racism and Sexism: An Integrated Study*. New York: St. Martin's Press.

Roudi-Fahimi, Farzaneh. 1988. "The Demography of Islam." *Population Today*, 16:3, 6–9.

Roudi-Fahimi, Farzaneh. 2002. "Iran's Family Planning Program: Responding to a Nation's Needs." Washington D.C.: Population Reference Bureau.

Roudi-Fahimi, Farzaneh. 2003. Women's Reproductive Health in the Middle East and North Africa. Washington D.C: Population Reference Bureau, February.

———. 2004. *Islam and Family Planning*. Washington D.C.: Population Reference Bureau. 2004.

Roudi-Fahimi, Farzaneh, and Mary Mederios Kent. 2007. *Challenges and Opportunities—the Population of the Middle East and North Africa*. Population Bulletin. Washington DC: Population Reference Bureau, vol. 62, no. 2.

Roudi-Fahimi, Farzaneh, and Valentine M. Moghadam. 2003. *Empowering Women, Developing Society: Female Education in the Middle East and North Africa*. Washington, D.C.: Population Reference Bureau, November.

Russell, J.C. 1958. Late Ancient and Medieval Population. *Transactions of the American Philosophical Society*, 48, part 3 (June).

Rustow, Dankwart, A. 1967. *A World of Nations: Problems of Political Modernization*. Washington, DC: The Brookings Institute, pp. 1–5.

Ryan, M.P. 1975. Womanhood in America: From Colonial Times to the Present. New York: New Viewpoints.

Safa, H.I. 1983. "Women, Production, and Reproduction in Industrial Capitalism: A Comparison of Brazilian and Untied States Factory Workers." *Women, Men and the International Division of Labor*. Eds. J. Nash and M.P. Fernandez-Kelly. Albany: State University of New York Press, pp. 95–116.

Safa, Helen. 2002. "Questioning Globalization: Gender and Export Processing in the Dominican Republic." *JDS*, 18:2–3, 11–31.

Said, Edward. 1993. *Culture and Imperialism*. New York: Knopf.

———. 1979. *Orientalism*. New York: Vintage Books.

Salaff, Janet. 1981. *Working Daughters of Hong Kong*. New York: Cambridge University Press.

Salehi-Isfahani, Djavad. 2000a. "Demographic Factors in Iran's Economic Development." *Social Research*, 67:2 (Summer), 599–620.

———. 2000b. "Microeconomics of Growth in MENA—the Role of Households." Global Research Project, Global Development Networks.

Sanderson, Stephen, and Arthur Alderson. 2005. *World Societies, the Evolution of Human Social Life*. Boston: Pearson Publishing Company.

Sarbib, Jean-Louis. "Building Knowledge Societies in the Middle East and North Africa." Knowledge for Development: A Forum for Middle East & North Africa, Palais du Pharo, Marseilles,

France, September 9, 2002. Retrieved on August 6, 2007, http://lnweb18.worldbank.org/mna/mena.nsf/Attachments/k4d+op-ed-Eng/$File/k4d+op-ed-English.pdf.

Sassen, Saskia. 1988. *The Mobility of Labor and Capital, A Study in International Investment and Labor Flow.* New York: Cambridge University Press.

————. 1999. *Losing Control: Sovereignty in an Age of Globalization.* New York: Columbia University Press.

————. 2007. *A Sociology of Globalization.* New York: Norton & Company.

Schultz, T. Paul. 1973. "Explanation of Birth Rate Changes over Space and Time: A Study of Taiwan." *Journal of Political Economy,* 81:2, part 2 (March/April), S238–274.

Semyonov, M. 1980. "The Social Context of Women's Labor Force Participation: A Comparative Analysis." *American Journal of Sociology,* 86, 534–550.

Semyonov, M., and Y. Shenhav. 1988. "Investment Dependence, Economic Development, and Female Opportunities in Less Developed Countries." *Social Science Quarterly,* 69, 961–978.

Sen, Amartya. 1999. *Development and Freedom.* Oxford: Oxford University Press.

Sen, G., and Caren Grown. 1987. *Development, Crises and Alternative Visions: Third World Women's Perspectives.* New York: Monthly Review Press.

Shah, Nasra M. 1995. "Structural Changes in the Receiving Country and Future Labor Migration-The Case of Kuwait." *International Migration Review,* 29:4 (Winter), 1000–1022.

Sharabi, Hisham. 1988. *Neopatriarchy: A Theory of Distorted Change in Arab Society.* New York: Oxford University Press.

Shavarini, Mitra. 2006. "Wearing the Veil to College: The Paradox of Higher Education in the Lives of Iranian Women." *International Journal of Middle East Studies,* 38, 189–211.

Simmons, John, and Russell A. Stone. 1976. *Change in Tunisia.* Albany: State University of New York Press.

Singh, Ram, D. 1994. "Fertility-mortality Variations across LDCs: Women's Education, Labor Force Participation, and Contraceptive Use." *Kyklos,* 47:2, 209–221.

Singh, S., and R. Samara. 1996. "Early Marriage among Women in Developing Countries." *International Family Planning Perspectives,* 22:4, 148–157, 175.

Sivard, R. 1985. *Women...A World Survey.* New York: Carnegie, Ford and Rockefeller Foundations.

Smith, Bonnie G. 2005. *Women's History in Global Perspective.* Urbana: University of Illinois Press.

Standing, Guy. 1981. *Labor Force Participation and Development.* Geneva: International Labor Organization.

Statistical Record of Women Worldwide. 1995. (2nd Ed.) New York: Gale Research.

Stowasser, Barbara. 1998. "Gender Issues in Contemporary Qur'anic Interpretation." *Islam, Gender, and Social Change.* Eds. Yvonne Yazbeck Haddad and John L. Esposito. New York: Oxford University Press, pp. 30–44.

Stromquist, Nelly P. 1997. "State Politics and Gender Equity: Comparative Perspectives." *Gender, Equity, and Schooling: Policy and Practice.* Eds. Barbara J. Bank and Peter M. Hall. New York: Garland Publishing, Inc.

Suk-Ching Ho. 1984. "Women's Labor Force Participation in Hong Kong 1971–1981." *Journal of Marriage and the Family,* 46: 4 (November), 947–953.

Sullivan, Michael J. 1991. *Measuring Global Values: The Ranking of 162 Countries.* New York: Greenwood Press.

Telhami, Shibley, Benjamin Smith, Michael Ross, and Steven Heydemann. 2009. *Oil, Globalization, and Political Reform.* The Brookings Project on U.S. Relations with the Islamic World, Doha Discussion Papers. 2009 U.S.-Islamic World Forum, Governance, Religion, and Politics Task Force. Washington, D.C.: Saban Center at Brookings.

Tertzakian, Peter. 2006. *A Thousand Barrels a Second: The Coming Oil Break Point and the Challenges Facing an Energy Dependent World.* New York: McGraw-Hill.

Tienda, Marta, and Rebecca Rajman. 1997. "Immigrants' income packaging and invisible labor force activity." Paper presented at the urban poverty workshop, Northwestern University and the University of Chicago.

Tilly, Louise A., and Joan W. Scott. 1978. *Women, Work and Family.* New York and London: Routledge.

Ting-Toomey, Stella. 1999. *Communicating Across Cultures.* New York: Guilford Press.

Tinker, Irene, ed. 1990. *Persistent Inequalities: Women and World Development.* New York: Oxford University Press.

UNDP, Arab Fund for Economic and Social Development. 2002. The Arab Human Development Report. *Creating Opportunities for Future Generations,* New York.

UNDP, Arab Fund for Economic and Social Development. 2005. The Arab Human Development Report. *Towards the Rise of Women in the Arab World.*

UNDP, Human Development Indicators, 2003. http://hdr.undp.org/reports/global/2003/indicator/indic_207_1_1.html.

UNDP, The Arab Human Development Report. 2005. Towards the Rise of Women in the Arab World. United Nations Development Programme, New York.

UN Development Fund for Women (UNIFEM). 2004. *Progress of Arab Women: One Paradigm, Four Arena, and more than 140 Million Women.* http://www.arabwomenconnect.org/docs/PAW2004-beginning.pdf.

UN Population Fund (UNFPA). 2002. *State of World Population 2002: People, Poverty, and Possibilities.* New York: UNFPA.

United Nations. 1982, 1989. *Demographic Yearbook.* Table 31. United Nations Publications.

———. 1982. *Energy Statistics Yearbook.* 1982. United Nations Publications.

———. 1984. *Improving Concepts and Methods for Statistics and Indicators on the Situation of Women.* New York: United Nations Department of International Economic and Social Affairs.

———. 1991. *The World's Women 1970–1990 Trends and Statistics.* Social Statistics and Indicators. Series K, no. 8. United Nations: New York.

United Nations Report. 2003. *World Population Policies.*

U.S. Library of Congress Country Studies. Retrieved on August 13, 2006, http://rs6.loc.gov/frd/cs/.

Van Der Lippe, Tanja, and Liset Van Dijk. 2002. "Comparative Research on Women's Employment." *Annual Review of Sociology*, 28, 221–241.

Van Eeghen, Willem, and Kouassi Soman. 1997. "Poverty in the Middle East and North Africa." Accessed online at www.worldbank.org/mdf/mdf1/menapoor.htm, on January 6, 2003.

Wahba, Jackline. 2003. "Women in MENA Labor Markets." Newsletter of the Economic Research Forum for the Arab Countries, Iran & Turkey. Vol. 10, no. 1 (Spring).

Wallerstein, Immanuel. 1974a. "The Rise and Future Demise of the World Capitalist System: Concepts for Comparative Analysis." *Comparative Studies in Society and History*, 16, 387–415.

———. 1974b. *The Modern World-System: Capitalist Agriculture and the Origins of the European World Economy in the Sixteenth Century.* New York: Academic Press.

Wallerstein, Immanuel. 1979. *The Capitalist World-Economy*. New York: Cambridge University Press.

———. 1980. *The Modern World-System, vol. II: Mercantilism and the Consolidation of the European World-Economy, 1600–1750*. New York: Academic Press.

———. 1984. *The Politics of the World Economy*. New York: Cambridge University Press.

———. 1989. *The Modern World-System, vol. III: The Second Great Expansion of the Capitalist World-Economy, 1730–1840's*. San Diego: Academic Press.

———. 1998. *Utopistics: Or Historical Changes of the Twenty-First Century*. New York: New Press.

Wallerstein, Immanuel, and Terence K. Hopkins. 1996. *The Age of Transition. Trajectories of the World System*. London: Zed Books.

Walter, W. 1981. *Women in Islam*. Montclair, NJ: Abner Schram.

Ward, K. 1984. *Women in the World System: Its Impact on Status and Fertility*. New York: Praeger.

Ward, Kathryn, ed. 1990. *Women Workers and Global Restructuring*. ILR Press: Cornell University.

Ware, H. 1981. *Women, Demography, and Development*. Canberra: Australian National University Press.

Weber, Max. [1994] 1958. *The Protestant Ethic and the Spirit of Capitalism*. Trans. by T. Parsons. Reprint, New York: Charles Scribner's Sons.

Weeks, John R. 1988. "The Demography of Islamic Nations." Population Reference Bureau. *Population Bulletin*, 43:4 (December).

Weinberger, Mary Beth, Cynthia Lloyd, and Ann K. Blanc. 1989. "Women's Education and Fertility: A Decade of Change in Four Latin American Countries." *International Family Planning Perspectives*, 15:1, 4–14.

Weiss, J., F. Ramirez, and T. Tracy. 1976. "Female Participation in the Occupational System: A Comparative Institutional Analysis." *Social Problems*, 23, 593–608.

Weller, Robert H., and Leon F. Bouvier. 1981. *Population, Demography & Policy*. New York: St. Martin Press.

Wilensky, Harold L. 1968. "Women's Work: Economic Growth, Ideology and Social Structure." *Industrial Relations*, 7, 235–248.

Willoughby, John. 2005. "A Quiet Revolution in the Making? The Replacement of Expatriate Labor through the Feminization of the Labor Force in GCC Countries." March 2005. Working Paper, Department of Economics Working Paper Series, American University. http://www.american.edu/cas/econ/workingpapers/2005–02.pdf. Retrieved on August 9, 2007.

Wolf, Diane L. 1990. "Linking Women's Labor with the Global Economy." *Women Workers and Global Restructuring*. Ed. Kathryn Ward. Ithaca, NY: ILR Press, pp. 1–22.

Women of Our World. 2002, 2005. *Population Reference Bureau*. Washington, D.C.

World Bank. 1983, 1987, and 1992. *World Development Report*. New York: Oxford University Press.

———. 1993. *Social Indicators of Development*. New York: Oxford University Press.

———. 1993. Diskette version. *Social Indicators of Development*. New York: Oxford University Press.

———. 1999. *Education in the Middle East and North Africa: A Strategy Towards Learning for Development*. Washington, D.C.: The World Bank.

———. 2000. *World Bank World Tables*. New York: Oxford University Press.

———. 2009. Global Economic Prospects 2009: Middle East and North Africa Regional Outlook.

World Bank Group. 2006. GenderStats database of gender statistics. Retrieved in August 12, 2006. http://devdata.worldbank.org/.

World Bank International Economic Department. 1993. World Tables of Economic and Social Indicators, 1950–1992 computer file. Washington D.C.

World Bank Social Indicators of Development. 1999. World Bank. Washington, D.C.

World Bank World Tables. 1993. World Bank. Washington, D.C.

World Development Indicators. 2005. Women in Development. World Bank.

World Population Data Sheet. 1990. *Population Reference Bureau*. Washington, D.C.

———. 2005. *Population Reference Bureau*. Washington, D.C.

———. 2007. *Population Reference Bureau*. Washington, D.C.

———. 2009. *Population Reference Bureau*. Washington, D.C.

World Resources Institute. *EarthTrends*, The Environmental Information Portal. Washington, D.C. http://www.EarthTrends.wri.org.

World Social Indicators of Development. 1993. The World Bank. Washington, D.C.

World's Women: Trends and Statistics. 1995, 2000. United Nations Statistics Division-Demographic, Social and Housing Statistics. United Nations: New York, http://www.unstats.un.org.

The World's Women 1970–1990 Trends and Statistics. 1991. Social Statistics and Indicators. Series K, No. 8. New York: United Nations.

Wrigley, E.A., Davies, R.S., Oeppen, J.E., and Ofield, R.S. 1997. *English Population History from Family Reconstitution 1580–1837.* Cambridge, UK: Cambridge University Press.

Yeganeh, Nahid. 1993. "Nationalism and National Identities." *Feminist Review*, no 44 (Summer), 3–18.

Young, K. 1988. *Women and Economic Development.* Oxford: Berg/UNESCO.

Youssef, Nadia H. 1974. *Women and Work in Developing Societies.* Berkeley: University of California Press.

———. 1978. "The Status and Fertility Patterns of Muslim Women." *Women in the Muslim World.* Eds. Lois Beck and Nikki Keddie. Cambridge, Massachusetts: Harvard University Press, pp. 69–99.

INDEX